CELEBRITY CHEFS

THIS BOOK IS DEDICATED TO OUR FRIEND AND HEALTHY-LIVING INSPIRATION, CHRISTINE WEBB.

CHRISTINE BEGAN WITH AN IDEA AND, WITH THE SAME DEDICATION SHE SHOWED TRAINING FOR THE IRONMAN
COMPETITION, WORKED TO MAKE THE ROCHESTER CELEBRITY COOKBOOK A REALITY.
THROUGH HER INFORMATIVE REPORTING, HER COMMITMENT TO THE COMMUNITY, AND HER PERSONAL EXAMPLE,
SHE SHOWS US ALL THAT THE LONGEST RACE BEGINS WITH THE FIRST HEALTHY STEP.

Proceeds from the sale of this book benefit the ESL Charitable Foundation, Unity Health Foundation, Arc of Monroe County, Gilda's Club of Rochester, and the Rochester City Ballet.

Art Direction, design, and layout by Sandy Knight and Gretchen Bye, Dixon Schwabl Advertising

Photography by Kurt Brownell Photography, unless otherwise noted

Written by Charles Benoit, Dixon Schwabl Advertising

Editing and proofreading by John Connelly, Dixon Schwabl Advertising

Production supervision by Christina Williams, Dixon Schwabl Advertising

Celebrity wrangling by Steve Dawe and Matt Basile

Kitchen sets kindly provided by Dell's House of Kitchens, Inc.

Nutritional analysis by Jean Bauch, R.D., C.D.E., and Grace Anne Ricci, M.S., R.D., C.D.N., Unity Health System

Monroe Litho, Inc., official printer of *Celebrity Chefs*

ISBN # 0-9711459-9-7

First Printing: October 2005

1 2 3 4 5 6 7 8 9 10

table of contents

INTRODUCTION

Welcome to the Celebrity Chefs Cookbook

Take 62 celebrities, add a team of renowned chefs, mix in important nutritional information, spice it up with Fun Foodie Facts and toast it all with the right wine and you've got a recipe for a great time. That's the idea behind *Celebrity Chefs Cookbook*—an exciting and informative volume filled with fast, easy, and delicious dishes designed to give every meal the star treatment. But what makes this collection of culinary classics truly special is how it helps support five inspiring charities right here in Rochester.

As the presenting sponsor of this cookbook, ESL Federal Credit Union continues its long-term commitment to the Greater Rochester community. Whether it's through the ESL Charitable Foundation, the underwriting of the ESL Jefferson Awards and ESL Stars for Seniors programs, or the sponsorship of such major events as the ESL International Air Show, ESL remains dedicated to making the Rochester region a vibrant, family-friendly place to live and work.

Co-sponsors Unity Health System and Rochester City Ballet were involved from the start, adding a unique blend of caring and creativity to the project. 13WHAM-TV and 1180 WHAM Radio lined up the celebrities who proved that they are just as comfortable in the kitchen as they are in the spotlight.

From savory soups and salads, exquisite appetizers and entrées, and desserts that redefine decadence, Tony Gullace and his team of chefs from Max of Eastman Place tried out each dish, determining just what was meant by "a pinch of this and that" and "garnish like they did in Spain," ensuring that every recipe was simple, tasty, and true.

Photographer Kurt Brownell brings his creative vision to the table with pictures that look good enough to eat, while the experts at Unity Health provide you with accurate nutritional information, allowing you to make the healthy choices that fit your lifestyle. The creative geniuses at Dixon Schwabl Advertising brought it all together, serving up a kitchen reference book you'll turn to time and again.

But the *Celebrity Chefs* cookbook does more than nourish your body; it nourishes your soul as well. By purchasing this book you are helping to support five important area charities. Proceeds from the sale of this book will be divided among the ESL Charitable Foundation, Unity Health Foundation, Arc of Monroe County, Gilda's Club of Rochester and the Rochester City Ballet. Call it the *pièce de résistance* that completes the meal.

So open up to any page and let's get cookin'!

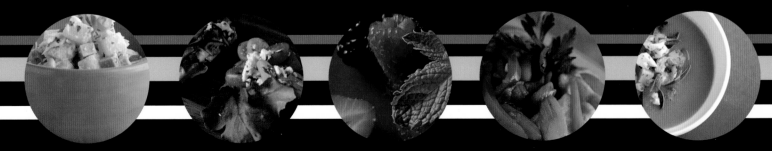

Can a financial institution actually inspire affection?

Happily, yes. Because providing personal touch service is our first priority. Always has been.
Always will be. Though we keep growing, we'll never lose touch with our roots. And that's a promise.

ESL
Federal Credit Union ®

It's banking, only better.

A nurse for 27 years,
SUSAN IS MOST PROUD OF
HER PATIENTS' EXPERIENCE.

HOW DO WE KNOW THAT UNITY PEOPLE PROVIDE
THE BEST HEALTH CARE EXPERIENCE? We ask.
We compile. And then we compare against
national benchmarks. You can see the results
in the Care to Compare section of our Web
site. And since our overall satisfaction rate
is 97.5%, we feel safe in saying Susan and her
co-workers measure up.

Unity Health System

www.unityhealth.org

6

FIERCELY PROVOCATIVE. GENTLY SUBLIME.

ROCHESTER
City Ballet

WWW.ROCHESTERCITYBALLET.COM

7

Takin' it to the Max

For Tony Gullace, owner and head chef at Max of Eastman Place, community service is one of the essential ingredients in a good life. So when he was asked to field test all 62 of the celebrity recipes in just four days, he was eager to help.

"With the people involved in this project I knew it would be fun," Tony says. "It's all about trying something new."

To give every recipe a triple look, Tony enlisted the help of his fellow Max chefs, Eric Mueller and Dan Martello.

"It's been a real eye-opener," says Eric. "Some of these recipes combined foods in ways I hadn't really thought of."

According to Eric, every recipe reflects the chef who created it. "Your more outgoing personalities often use zesty spices and dramatic presentations. With more reserved and quiet folks, you tend to see crockpots and traditional ingredients."

For Dan, cooking is all about self expression. "Recipes are not set in stone. You should always give a dish your own twist. Maybe it's a certain flavor or the way you garnish. But make it yours. Variety is what makes cooking so much fun."

All three chefs agree that working with photographer Kurt Brownell was a rare treat. "Things are busy in the kitchen," says Eric. "There's not a lot of time to stand around and admire your work. With Kurt's photos, the food looks as good as it tastes."

"People are really going to enjoy this cookbook," Tony says as he adds the finishing touches to another celebrity dish. "Me? I look forward to chatting with each of these celebrities the next time they're at Max. Who knows—they may have another recipe to share."

Tony's Secret Food Indulgence: Grilled Cheese

Eric's Secret Food Indulgence: Ice Cream

Dan's Secret Food Indulgence: "Depends on my mood, but you can't go wrong with mom's Sunday cooking."

MAX OF EASTMAN PLACE

What's Cookin' on WHAM...

The WHAM Morning News
with Chet Walker & Beth Adams
Weekdays 5am - 9am

The Glenn Beck Show
Weekdays 9am - 11am

The Bob Lonsberry Show
Weekdays 11am - 2pm

Rush Limbaugh
Weekdays 2pm - 5pm

The WHAM 5 O'clock News Hour
with Joe Lomonaco
Weekdays 5pm - 6pm

Talk Sports
with Bob Matthews
Weeknights 6pm - 8pm

1180
WHAM

The Savage Nation
with Michael Savage
8pm - 11pm

Sean Hannity
Weeknights 11pm - 1am

Say Cheese! And pasta and beef and pastry and wine...

Every job comes with its own rewards, and for Kurt Brownell, the photographer for the *Celebrity Chefs* Cookbook, the rewards were mighty tasty. Not only did Kurt capture the culinary beauty of every dish created by Tony Gullace and his team, he got to sample them all.

"It was a definite plus," says Kurt. "But it was also great going home each day from the shoot creatively and physically exhausted, knowing I'd produced images that would benefit not just one, but five different groups. That definitely made the hard work worth it."

Kurt's creativity and artistic vision have made him one of the area's most sought after photographers, yet even with his vast and varied experience, *Celebrity Chefs* offered something new. "I loved the challenge of creating a cohesive body of portraits and still-lifes in an incredibly short time and solving problems on the go."

When he's not tackling exciting photographic projects, Kurt enjoys traveling with his wife Liz and hanging out with their four cats and their dog, Loki.

"When you like to eat and drink as much as I do, running a couple of miles a day and working out never hurts. Of course, we're expecting our first child," Kurt says, laughing. "I'm sure these activities will change come January."

Kurt's Secret Food Indulgence: I don't have any secret food indulgences. I just indulge.

Kurt Brownell Photography creates images for a wide variety of commercial and editorial clients across the country. The man behind the lens for Dixon Schwabl Advertising's *Horses on Parade*, *Animal Scramble* and *Great Homes of Rochester*, Kurt Brownell Photography is based in Rochester. You can contact Kurt at kurtbrownell@rochester.rr.com, (585) 340-2372.

KURT
BROWNELL
PHOTOGRAPHY

Charles Benoit
Copywriter / busboy
On tap and on key, Charles'
words really sink in.

Jane Argenta
Public Relations Supervisor /
pastry chef
In and out of the kitchen, Jane
knows how to mix it up.

Howie Jacobson
Managing Partner / dishwasher
Whatever Howie's cooking, it's
toujours magnifique!

Sandy Knight
Design Team / photo stylist /
sous-chef
Measure for measure, Sandy
adds an extra large dose of
creativity.

Gretchen Bye
Design Team / dessert topper
Here's the scoop—Gretchen
is the design team's very own
spice girl.

Barbara Pierce
Director of Public Relations /
bartender
Barbara knows how to whet
the media's appetite for a
great story.

Mike Schwabl
Vice President / Maître d'
Mike puts fun—and ice
cream—back on the menu.

Lauren Dixon
CEO / Hostess
It all starts with Lauren's
secret recipe for success.

Jessica Savage
Account Executive /
party planner
Jessica dishes out
excitement and serves it up
with a side of style.

Susan Clevenger
Producer / hat-check girl
A real flour-child, Susan
brings all the ingredients
together.

Christina Williams
Production Supervisor /
sommelier
It's bound to be great when
Christina is involved.

David Lyttle
CFO / bouncer
From account books to
cookbooks, David's on the
money.

John Connelly
Editor / food taster
Make no mistake, if it's not
right, John sends it back to
the kitchen.

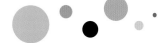

A Baker's Dozen *from*

DIXON SCHWABL ADVERTISING

From soup to nuts, this crew put it all on the table
to bring you the *Celebrity Chefs* cookbook.

1595 Moseley Road, Victor, New York 14564   585.383.0380
www.DixonSchwabl.com

12

THE CHARITIES

All proceeds from the *Celebrity Chefs* cookbook will benefit the following charities:

ESL Charitable Foundation – With more than 85 years serving the Rochester area, ESL Federal Credit Union has earned a reputation for meaningful community involvement and civic leadership. The ESL Charitable Foundation provides funding and employee volunteers to selected non-profit organizations, with a primary focus on families, youth and education.

Unity Health Foundation – supports the programs and services provided by Unity Health System from its Park Ridge Hospital Campus in the town of Greece, the Unity St. Mary's Campus in Rochester, and sites throughout Monroe County. The Foundation helps fund health and outreach programs for low-income and uninsured adults and children, as well as a comprehensive range of services and housing options for older adults.

Arc of Monroe County – works with and for individuals with developmental disabilities and their families. Arc of Monroe County offers a variety of services designed to increase independence and self-sufficiency, improve the quality of life, and enhance the self-esteem of program participants by providing meaningful social development, employment, community living, and enrichment opportunities.

Gilda's Club of Rochester – provides a meeting place where those living with cancer and their families and friends can join with others to build emotional and social support as a supplement to medical care. Gilda's Club also offers networking groups, lectures, workshops, and social events in a nonresidential, homelike setting.

Rochester City Ballet – helps keep the arts alive by presenting a full season of quality dance to diverse audiences, with performances that educate and entertain adults and children at community events and special Rochester City Ballet performances, creating more than 20 new critically-acclaimed ballets to complement its popular traditional repertoire.

LET'S EAT!

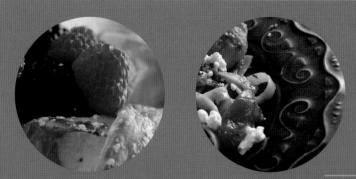

INGREDIENTS

1 head escarole

½ teaspoon minced garlic,
    or to taste

1 tablespoon olive oil

1 20 oz. jar or can chicken stock

1 16 oz. can Great Northern beans

Salt to taste

Sides:

Grated cheddar

Sour cream

Bread bowl

Tostitos®

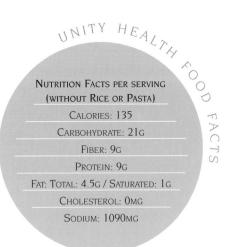

UNITY HEALTH FOOD FACTS

NUTRITION FACTS PER SERVING
(WITHOUT RICE OR PASTA)

CALORIES: 135

CARBOHYDRATE: 21G

FIBER: 9G

PROTEIN: 9G

FAT: TOTAL: 4.5G / SATURATED: 1G

CHOLESTEROL: 0MG

SODIUM: 1090MG

WHAT TO TOAST WITH

Robert
Mondavi
Fume
Blanc

Greens and Beans

serves 4

WHATCHA GOTTA DO...

Lightly sauté garlic in non-stick pan. Quickly add shredded escarole and then pour in chicken stock. Let this cook for several minutes before adding beans (include juice). When escarole is tender (about 5 minutes), drain fluid and season to taste. This can be served over rice or pasta, or alone as a side dish.

Beth Adams

1180 WHAM Radio Co-Host,
WHAM Morning News

Why is this your favorite healthy entrée recipe?

My friend, Mary Ann, made greens and beans for my late friend Bill Klein's birthday party. I dreamed about it for weeks afterwards and came up with my own version.

What is your fitness regime?

I try to stay fairly active by walking 4 to 5 miles a day (outdoors when possible). I also play tennis, bicycle, roller skate, and ice skate.

What is your secret food indulgence?

Fresh blueberries and watermelon! I can eat them by the gallon.

15

Alhart Pasta with Vegetables

serves 4-6

INGREDIENTS

2-3 tablespoons olive oil
1 large onion, chopped
2 cloves of garlic, chopped
1 14 oz. package of frozen broccoli or
   equivalent fresh
1 bag of baby carrots

1 14½ oz. can of chicken broth
1 teaspoon salt
½ teaspoon Italian seasoning
½-1 teaspoon dry basil
1 lb. pasta
Reggiano Parmesan cheese

WHATCHA GOTTA DO...

Cook vegetables separately. Sautée onion in olive oil until golden. Then add garlic—until lightly brown. Add chicken broth and seasonings. Simmer for about 5 minutes. Cook pasta separately. Add the cooked vegetables to the broth mixture and simmer until pasta is ready. After the pasta is drained, add to it vegetable mixture. Sprinkle with reggiano Parmesan cheese. Serve.

Cook time: 45 minutes

WHAT TO TOAST WITH

Franciscan
Cuvée
Sauvage

UNITY HEALTH FOOD FACTS

NUTRITION FACTS PER SERVING
(1/4 RECIPE)
CALORIES: 370
CARBOHYDRATE: 64G
FIBER: 5G
PROTEIN: 15G
FAT: TOTAL: 7G / SATURATED: 1.5G
CHOLESTEROL: 0MG
SODIUM: 670MG

Don Alhart

13WHAM News Anchor/
Associate News Director

Why is this your favorite healthy entrée recipe?

This was always a favorite of the kids when growing up. It is my wife, Mary's recipe, reflecting her Italian heritage, and brings back memories of family fellowship around the dinner table. It is something that can be made on short notice, with ingredients in the pantry and freezer.

What is your fitness regime?

I run 2½ miles, six days a week. I don't set any world records, usually accomplishing this task in 27-30 minutes. It is enough to increase my heartbeat to a good "workout" range. I also try to work out with weights—CYBEX—at least two days a week.

What is your secret food indulgence?

Vanilla-frosted sugar cookies.

Susan Ashline

1180 WHAM Radio
News Reporter/Anchor

Why is this your favorite healthy entrée recipe?

Everyone loves pizza and it's so easy to make!

Why is this your fitness regime?

My 10-year old accompanies me on evening walks as I push my toddler in a stroller. I have various exercise machines in my home that I use frequently and I regularly lift free weights. I don't buy junk food and I don't buy foods that are high in fat and/or cholesterol.

What is your secret food indulgence?

Pizza. I could eat it seven days a week—for breakfast, lunch or dinner, or all of the above.

INGREDIENTS

1 Boboli® crust
1 cup pizza sauce
¼ teaspoon salt
⅛ teaspoon pepper
2 cups fresh mushrooms, chopped
1 cup small broccoli florets
½ cup chopped green peppers
½ cup chopped green onions
1 cup shredded mozzarella

Veggie Pizza

WHATCHA GOTTA DO...

Steam mushrooms and broccoli but do not over cook. Preheat oven to 400. Spread sauce over crust. Top with all remaining ingredients. Sprinkle cheese on top. Bake for 20 to 25 minutes until crust is golden brown.

WHAT TO TOAST WITH

Ruffino Chianti

Lemon Chicken by Rachael Ray

serves 4

INGREDIENTS

1 ½ lbs. chicken breast or chicken tenders, cut
    into chunks

¼ cup all-purpose unbleached flour

Coarse salt

2 tablespoons wok or vegetable oil, 2 turns of the
    pan (preferred brand: House of Tsang®)

1 tablespoon (a splash) white or
    rice wine vinegar

½ cup chicken broth or stock

8 ozs. (1 cup) prepared lemon curd

¼ cup hot water

1 lemon, zested

2 scallions, thinly sliced or 20 blades fresh
    chives, finely chopped

WHATCHA GOTTA DO...

Coat the chunked chicken lightly with flour, season with a little salt. Heat a large skillet or a wok-shaped nonstick pan over high heat. Stir-fry chicken until golden, 3 or 4 minutes. Remove chicken from the pan and return pan to heat, reduce to medium. Add a splash of vinegar to the pan and let it evaporate. Add stock or broth to pan and scrape up drippings with a whisk. Thin curd by stirring in a little hot water. Add curd to broth and whisk to combine. Add chicken back to the pan and simmer for 1 to 2 minutes to thicken sauce and finish cooking chicken pieces through. Remove the pan from heat, add the scallions or chives and zest, and toss chicken pieces well to combine zest and scallions or chives evenly throughout the sauces. Serve over rice.

Cook's notes: Wok oil infused with ginger and garlic is usually available on the International Food aisle in many markets. Chicken broths and stocks are available in resealable paper containers, making storage of remaining product easy to keep on hand in the refrigerator; they are found in the soup aisle. Lemon curd is a sweet lemon spread available in most markets; it is on the jam/jelly aisle.

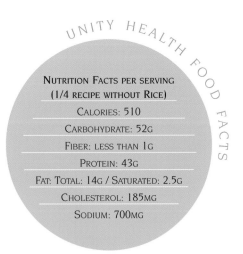

UNITY HEALTH FOOD FACTS

NUTRITION FACTS PER SERVING
(1/4 RECIPE WITHOUT RICE)

CALORIES: 510

CARBOHYDRATE: 52G

FIBER: LESS THAN 1G

PROTEIN: 43G

FAT: TOTAL: 14G / SATURATED: 2.5G

CHOLESTEROL: 185MG

SODIUM: 700MG

Glenn Beck

1180 WHAM Radio Talk Show Host

Why is this your favorite healthy entrée recipe?

Reminds me of the kids—we love to cook this together on our family home evenings.

What is your fitness regime?

Walk to the ice cream store.

What is your secret food indulgence?

It's no secret—Cold Stone Creamery®.

INGREDIENTS

1 lb. ricotta cheese

1½ cup sugar

2 tablespoons flour

2 tablespoon lemon juice

1 stick of butter

Graham crackers

1 16 oz. package cream cheese

4 eggs

2 tablespoons cornstarch

2 tablespoons vanilla

16 oz. sour cream

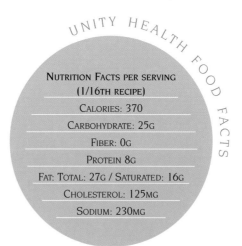

UNITY HEALTH FOOD FACTS

NUTRITION FACTS PER SERVING
(1/16TH RECIPE)

CALORIES: 370

CARBOHYDRATE: 25G

FIBER: 0G

PROTEIN 8G

FAT: TOTAL: 27G / SATURATED: 16G

CHOLESTEROL: 125MG

SODIUM: 230MG

Aunt Rose Caruso's
Cheesecake

WHATCHA GOTTA DO...

Preheat oven to 350 degrees. Break up graham crackers and strain to flour consistency. Butter 9¾" push-up pan and coat with graham crackers. Melt butter and cool. Separate egg yolks and whites. Blend cream cheese and ¼ cup sugar. Add ricotta. Blend each item as you go along. Gradually add sugar after each item is added. Add egg yolks, one at a time. Add flour, lemon juice, vanilla, and cornstarch. Add the rest of the butter. Add sour cream. Beat egg whites till foamy and fold in. Bake for 1 hour. Leave in the oven for two hours longer. Cool and refrigerate.

Joy Behar

ABC TV's "The View" Co-Host

Liz Bonis

1180 WHAM Radio/13WHAM News
Health Team Reporter

Why is this your favorite healthy entrée recipe?

It's in one pot, is easy to prepare, gets better as it sits, and makes a great low-fat home-cooked dinner date dish that doesn't taste low in fat!

What is your fitness regime?

Those early morning treadmill workouts at 3am—at least 30 minutes of cardio plus resistance training most days of the week. Add an evening walk and you have a real stress reducer too!

What is your secret food indulgence?

Popcorn, lots of it . . . with butter of course . . . and I always have chocolate kisses at home (are there any other kind?)

Winter White

NUTRITION FACTS PER SERVING
(1/4 RECIPE WITHOUT RICE)

CALORIES: 329

CARBOHYDRATE: 49G

FIBER: 11G

PROTEIN: 19G

FAT: TOTAL: 7G / SATURATED: 4G

CHOLESTEROL: 32MG

SODIUM: 484MG

INGREDIENTS

1 9 oz. package of fresh four-cheese
    ravioli
1 15 or 16 oz. can of Great Northern or
    navy beans, rinsed and drained
1 14.5 oz. can of diced tomatoes,
    undrained
$\frac{1}{2}$ teaspoon dried basil

$\frac{1}{2}$ teaspoon dried oregano
$\frac{1}{8}$ teaspoon crushed red pepper
6 cups of chopped escarole or spinach
    (yes, green, leafy vegetables!!)
$\frac{1}{4}$ cup of water
$\frac{1}{4}$ cup (1 oz.) grated Asiago cheese

WHATCHA GOTTA DO...

Cook pasta according to package directions; do not add salt or fat. Combine the beans, tomatoes, basil oregano, and red pepper in a large saucepan. Bring to a boil; stir in escarole. Cover, reduce heat, and simmer 3 minutes or until escarole is wilted. Stir in pasta and $\frac{1}{4}$ cup of water, cook 1 minute or until thoroughly heated. Sprinkle with cheese.

WHAT TO TOAST WITH

Ruffino
Chianti

RUFFINO

CHIANTI

2004

Maggie Brooks

MONROE COUNTY EXECUTIVE

Why is this your favorite healthy entrée recipe?

It's easy to make and it doesn't take a lot of prep time. In fact, you can make it ahead of time and reheat when you're ready to serve. It's ideal for those with busy schedules.

What is your fitness regime?

It's hard to make healthy living a priority with my busy schedule at work and at home. I try to allow time to work out on my treadmill for 20 minutes, three times a week. I also try to eat healthy foods, limit carbohydrates, and focus on portion size.

What is your secret food indulgence?

An occasional cheeseburger and fries. Occasionally!

INGREDIENTS

1 lb. package of boneless, skinless chicken breasts
1 can 98% fat-free cream of mushroom soup
1 10 oz. package low-fat shredded cheese or cheese slices
1 10 oz. package frozen chopped broccoli
¼ cup milk
Crushed croutons (optional)

serves 4

Chicken Divan

WHATCHA GOTTA DO...

Cut chicken into bite-size pieces. Brown in a small amount of oil in frying pan, set aside.
Spray medium-sized casserole dish with non-stick cooking spray. Layer bottom of dish
with frozen broccoli (no need to thaw). Layer chicken on top of broccoli. Cover chicken with
shredded cheese or cheese slices. Mix cream of mushroom soup with milk. Pour
over casserole ingredients. Sprinkle with crushed croutons, if desired. Bake at
350 degrees until heated through.

Cook time: Approximately 45 minutes

WHAT TO TOAST WITH

Nobilo
Marlborough
Sauvignon
Blanc

Gorgonzola Stuffed Filet Mignon

serves 2

INGREDIENTS

1 lb. filet mignon
12 oz. shredded gorgonzola
1 package McCormick® brown sauce mix

1 large portobello mushroom
1 12 oz. can of Genny® Light beer

WHATCHA GOTTA DO...

This recipe is ideal for cooking on your grill, especially if you have a side burner. In a skillet, on your side burner, add one cup of water and the 12 oz. can of Genny® Light, set on low. Finely chop the portobello mushroom and add to skillet. Slowly mix in the packaged brown sauce. Cover the skillet and stir frequently on low heat. Allow to simmer while cooking the meat. Butterfly the filet mignon leaving one side intact. Bring the grill temp to high. Sear the steak on both sides, reduce heat to low and cook for 15 minutes, turning once. When the meat is just about done, place 8 oz. of shredded gorgonzola cheese in the middle of the meat halves. Close the grill cover and finish cooking. Put the remaining 4 oz. of cheese in the skillet with the brown sauce and stir. Place the filet on a plate and pour the sauce over the top. Enjoy!

Cook time: about 20 minutes, cooked on the backyard grill and side burner or in broiler on high.

WHAT TO TOAST WITH

Franciscan
Magnificant

UNITY HEALTH FOOD FACTS

NUTRITION FACTS PER SERVING
(8 OZ. FILET MIGNON PER PERSON)

CALORIES: 1200

CARBOHYDRATE: 8G

FIBER: LESS THAN 1G

PROTEIN: 81G

FAT: TOTAL: 84G / SATURATED: 45G

CHOLESTEROL: 275MG

SODIUM: 2800MG

John Carr

1180 WHAM Radio Co-host,
WHAM Home Repair Clinic,
Managing Partner, Vision Sales, Inc.

Why is this your favorite healthy entrée recipe?

A variation of this recipe was discovered while out to dinner with good friends at my favorite restaurant. I have enjoyed this low-carb meal for many years and have adapted it to my own taste.

What is your fitness regime?

I run and occasionally lift weights to keep my weight down and stay fit and trim. I usually keep to a low-carbohydrate diet.

What is your secret food indulgence?

Potato chips and Buffalo calamari.

NUTRITION FACTS PER SERVING
(1/4 RECIPE)

CALORIES: 560

CARBOHYDRATE: 7G

FIBER: 0G

PROTEIN: 34G

FAT: TOTAL: 45G / SATURATED: 13G

CHOLESTEROL: 150MG

SODIUM: 430MG

WHAT TO TOAST WITH

Heron Hill
Dry Riesling

Tilapia with capers

serves 4

INGREDIENTS

Tilapia recipe ingredients:

1½ lbs. fillet of tilapia
Flour for coating
2 tablespoons canola oil
3 tablespoons unsalted butter

Black Butter and Olive Oil
Sauce Recipe Ingredients:

3 tablespoons unsalted butter
3 tablespoons olive oil
2 tablespoons balsamic vinegar
⅓ cup capers

Wendell Castle

ARTIST

Why is this your favorite healthy entrée recipe?
It tastes delicious and it's healthy.

What is your fitness regime?
Physical work and tennis three times a week, year-round.

What is your secret food indulgence?
Vic & Irv's onion rings!

WHATCHA GOTTA DO...

Dredge tilapia in flour, making sure it is evenly coated on both sides. Heat butter and canola oil in a large iron skillet. Sauté the fish for two to three minutes on each side, or until done and golden. Meanwhile, in a small skillet over medium heat, melt butter with olive oil. Drop in capers and fry. Add the vinegar and stir. Pour sauce over fish and serve immediately.

Cook time: 8 to 10 minutes

Mike Catalana

13WHAM Sports Director

Why is this your favorite healthy entrée recipe?

I love pasta. I grew up eating pasta all the time. My wife Bernadette knew that and used this dish to get me to eat a lot of things I never ate when I was younger. She always makes little changes (like the shrimp) to make it better each time.

What is your fitness regime?

I go to the gym on a regular basis to try and stay in shape. Plus I play basketball two to three times a week and try my best to keep up with the young guys.

What is your secret food indulgence?

Chips and salsa (I know the salsa is not the problem).

INGREDIENTS

1 16 oz. can diced tomatoes
1/4 teaspoon crushed red pepper
2 tablespoons olive oil
1 6 oz. sliced mushrooms
3/4 cup of quartered sun-dried
    tomatoes
1/8 cup of dried basil
1 crushed garlic clove
1/4 cup butter
3/4 cup of half and half
1/2 cup vodka
Shrimp (optional)
1 lb. pasta

Pasta with a Punch

serves 4
(6 as side)

WHATCHA GOTTA DO...

Melt butter in large heavy skillet over medium high heat. Add diced
tomatoes with their juices, half and half, vodka, and red pepper. Simmer
for 8 minutes. Shrimp can be added at this time if pre-cooked. In
another skillet, heat oil and sauté mushrooms for 4 minutes. Add sun-
dried tomatoes, artichoke hearts, and crushed garlic. Sauté 2 minutes
more. Add to other sauce and cook for 5 minutes. While cooking other
ingredients, boil linguine to desired doneness. Then toss sauce and
basil with cooked pasta of your choice.

Cook time: 25 minutes

WHAT TO TOAST WITH

Ruffino
Chianti

RUFFINO

CHIANTI

2004

INGREDIENTS

4 steaks
½ dark chocolate bar
1 tablespoon chili powder
1 tablespoon black pepper
½ cup fresh ground coffee

NUTRITION FACTS PER SERVING
(1/4 RECIPE)

CALORIES: 450

CARBOHYDRATE: 4G

FIBER: 0G

PROTEIN 42G

FAT: TOTAL: 29G / SATURATED: 12G

CHOLESTEROL: 95MG

SODIUM: 115MG

WHAT TO TOAST WITH

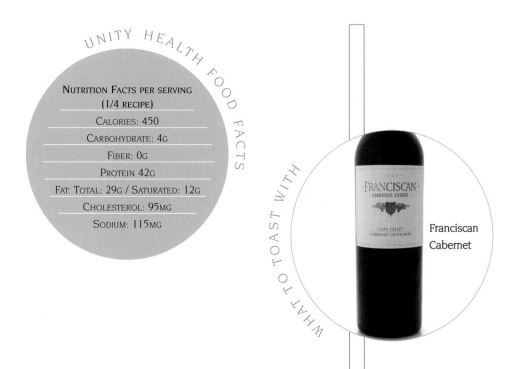

Franciscan
Cabernet

Chocolate-Coffee Steak

serves 4

WHATCHA GOTTA DO...

Grind coffee and mix with chili powder, black pepper, and shaved chocolate in small bowl. Tenderize steaks and rub in dry marinade. Sear both sides quickly on the grill to melt the chocolate. Grill to preference. Great with grilled asparagus spears!

Kyle Clark

13WHAM NEWS REPORTER

Why is this your favorite healthy entrée recipe?

Chocolate-Coffee Steak was stumbled upon by six guys at Ithaca College with a grill and way too much free time.

What is your fitness regime?

In addition to chasing down stories, I'm always looking to get in time on the tennis courts, indoor or outside, all year long.

What is your secret food indulgence?

I'll drive home to Lyons for my mother's homemade coffeecake, anytime.

Rosemary Shrimp and Artichoke Pasta

serves 4

INGREDIENTS

1 lb. uncooked medium-size shrimp
2 tablespoons olive oil
3 tablespoons butter
1 tablespoon fresh rosemary leaves
pasta

WHATCHA GOTTA DO...

Remove shrimp casings and veins under cold running water and let drain in colander. Heat olive oil and butter over medium heat and stir in fresh rosemary leaves and shrimp. Cook gently until shrimp turns pink (4-6 minutes). Serve over favorite pasta (sometimes use artichoke pasta in place of wheat pasta).
Cook time: 4-6 minutes

Serving size: 8-10 shrimp over medium mound of pasta
This is good served with fresh asparagus and a tomato and fresh basil salad with a light sprinkle of olive oil and balsamic vinegar.

For dessert I like my "Minimal Mousse." I make Jello (non-sugar) and pour it in the blender while still liquid and add 8 oz. of plain, non-fat yogurt. When blended, pour into serving dish and refrigerate. Serve with any fresh fruit!

UNITY HEALTH FOOD FACTS

NUTRITION FACTS PER SERVING
(1/4 RECIPE WITHOUT PASTA)

CALORIES:	260
CARBOHYDRATE:	1G
FIBER:	0G
PROTEIN:	23G
FAT: TOTAL: 17G / SATURATED: 7G	
CHOLESTEROL:	195MG
SODIUM:	250MG

WHAT TO TOAST WITH

twin fin
CALIFORNIA
chardonnay

Twin Fin
California
Chardonnay

Charlotte Clarke

13WHAM-TV Community Affairs Director

Why is this your favorite healthy entrée recipe?

My favorite neighbor, Marie, whose parents came to America from Sicily, shared this with me. It's super fast, easy and delicious! The olive oil addition helps with the butter cholesterol count and it still tastes great! It must be good for your heath; Marie is 83 and still going strong! The rosemary is what gives it a distinctive taste.

What is your fitness regime?

I live near the Erie Canal, so I walk on the canal path or around the block checking out everybody's flower gardens. I've got a little bouncy trampoline which I use sporadically and a yoga routine—which I do occasionally. The most consistent exercise I get is running upstairs to the bedroom and downstairs to the laundry room. I purposely build in extra trips! My favorite form of exercise is dancing. You can't beat Marvin Gaye or South Africa's Miriam Makeba to get you moving!

What is your secret food indulgence?

A hot, crusty French roll with sweet butter and a cup of coffee on a Sunday morning!

INGREDIENTS

Toast 8 tablespoons of slivered
  almonds and 2 tablespoons of
  sesame seeds
8 green onions, chopped
1 package of Ramen noodles
2 cooked chicken breasts (shredded)
1 package coleslaw

Dressing:
½ cup peanut oil
6 tablespoon of rice vinegar
1 teaspoon salt
1 teaspoon pepper
1 tablespoon sugar
1 teaspoon Accent® seasoning

UNITY HEALTH FOOD FACTS

NUTRITION FACTS PER SERVING (1/8 RECIPE)	
CALORIES: 280	
CARBOHYDRATE: 12G	
FIBER: 3G	
PROTEIN: 10G	
FAT: TOTAL: 21G / SATURATED: 3.5G	
CHOLESTEROL: 20MG	
SODIUM: 580MG	

serves 8

Chinese Chicken Salad

Brad & Amy Davies

1180 WHAM RADIO SPORTS DIRECTOR
SPORTS TALK HOST, HOT TALK 1280 WHTK

Why is this your favorite healthy entrée recipe?

I must admit to never having a favorite HEALTHY entrée until I met my wife. I LOVE her Chinese Chicken Salad (which is a recipe stolen from her mom, Karen!)

What is your fitness regime?

My wife and I like to take long walks (and short runs) with our basset hound Bogie four or five times per week.

What is your secret food indulgence?

Anything that starts out RED and cooks on the grill!

WHATCHA GOTTA DO...

Mix salad and ingredients.
Add dressing.
Top with noodles just before serving.

WHAT TO TOAST WITH

Heron Hill
Johannisberg
Riesling

Gail's Healthy Cookies

INGREDIENTS

½ cup butter, softened
½ cup almond butter
1 ¼ cups brown sugar
½ cup white sugar
2 eggs
1 teaspoon vanilla extract
½ teaspoon almond extract
1 cup flour
3 cups oatmeal
1 teaspoon baking soda
1 tablespoon ground flaxseed
1 teaspoon wheat germ

WHATCHA GOTTA DO...

Preheat oven to 350 degrees.
Combine all ingredients.
Drop onto cookie sheet.

Bake at 350 degrees
for 10 minutes

Evan Dawson

13WHAM NEWS REPORTER

Why is this your favorite healthy entrée recipe?
The flaxseed and wheat germ provide health benefits, and you can't even taste them. Our friends enjoy these cookies because they're so easy to make, and they're relatively guilt-free. We've amended this recipe slightly, which is named for its creator, our good friend Gail.

Flaxseed contains lignans. These phytoestrogens may help prevent breast cancer, prostate cancer, and endometrial cancer. Flaxseed also contains both soluble fiber, which helps lower cholesterol and regulates blood sugar, and insoluble fiber, which may help protect against colon cancer. It also has Omega-3 fatty acids that help lower the risk of cardiovascular disease and stroke.

This is my favorite recipe because it's a better alternative to giving in to my sweet tooth and eating junk food or chocolate. My wife and I are cursed with a love for sweets, but instead of eating foods that are high in trans fats and other garbage, we can enjoy a cookie that actually provides some health benefits.

What is your fitness regime?
I like to jog, and I often jog through the surrounding neighborhoods. I also do crunches and I work out with a curl bar at home. On top of that, I try to play recreational sports. When I play golf, I walk as much as I can.

What is your secret food indulgence?
I don't think it's a secret—when we don't have a batch of Gail's Healthy Cookies around, I tend to give in to chocolate of some sort. That's why we try not to keep much chocolate in the house!

Nutrition Facts per serving
(1/36 recipe)

Calories: 130

Carbohydrate: 18g

Fiber: 1g

Protein: 2g

Fat: Total: 5g / Saturated: 2g

Cholesterol: 20mg

Sodium: 70mg

Breakfast Sandwiches

serves 1 - 2

INGREDIENTS

Sliced ham
2 eggs
Butter
Cheese slices
Bagels or English muffins

WHATCHA GOTTA DO...

Split open two bagels or English muffins, put ham on one side of each, cheese on the other side, place in microwave. Fry two eggs, sunny side up. When it's time to flip the eggs, microwave the other ingredients for 30 seconds. Break the yolk of the eggs with a spatula, flip, remove from heat. Take muffins or bagels out of microwave, put eggs on the cheese side. The softened cheese and the yolk mix together—making a moist sandwich but not one too runny to hold on to.

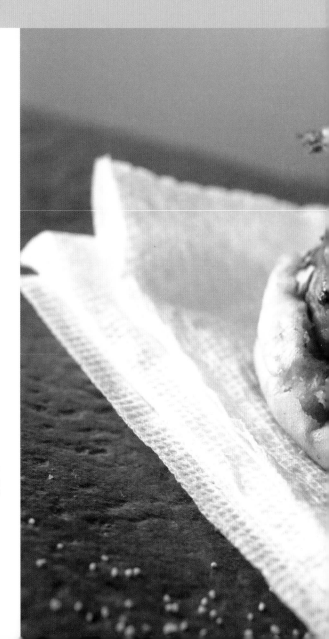

UNITY HEALTH FOOD FACTS

NUTRITION FACTS PER SERVING
(1/2 RECIPE)

CALORIES: 520 (BAGEL); 350 (MUFFIN)

CARBOHYDRATE: 62G; 29G

FIBER: 3G; 2G

PROTEIN: 27G; 20G

FAT: TOTAL: 17G; 16G / SATURATED: 6G; 6G

CHOLESTEROL: 240MG; 240MG

SODIUM: 1380MG; 1050MG

Mike DiGiorgio

1180 WHAM RADIO ENTERTAINMENT CRITIC
EXECUTIVE PRODUCER: WHAM MORNING NEWS/BOB LONSBERRY SHOW

Why is this your favorite healthy entrée recipe?

I love breakfast food, but don't always have time to make it. And very few places put breakfast sandwiches on their menus 24 hours a day. For me, at lunch time it's great to have breakfast food AND a sandwich.

What is your fitness regime?

Right now, I only get exercise racking my brain trying to think of an exercise regime. I'll have to see what my colleagues recommend. After all, I'm the guy who picked a breakfast sandwich as the healthiest food I cook.

What is your secret food indulgence?

Kraft Easy Cheese and crackers. Easy Cheese is the spray stuff that comes in a tube. A lot of people call that Cheez Whiz, but that's just wrong. Cheez Whiz is a spread. With Easy Cheese, you don't even dirty a knife. Just grab a package of Ritz crackers, a tube of Easy Cheese and relax in front of the TV!

Oyster Sauce & Catsup Marinade
Mashed Potatoes and Brussel

INGREDIENTS

Oyster Sauce and Catsup Marinade recipe ingredients:

Oyster sauce

Catsup

1 garlic clove

Mashed Potato recipe ingredients:

White potatoes

Skim milk

Pat of butter

3 tablespoons horseradish

Brussel Sprouts recipe ingredients:

Brussel sprouts, sliced

1 tablespoon sugar

Extra Virgin Olive Oil

1 1/2 garlic cloves

Parsley

Salt and Pepper
*   to taste*

WHATCHA GOTTA DO...

Marinade recipe instructions: Mix together oyster sauce and catsup. Cut slices into the top of the sirloin steak and insert garlic clove pieces. Marinade the steak in the prepared sauce for as long as you like. Broil in the oven for 10 minutes and you're ready to eat!

Mashed Potato recipe instructions: Boil potatoes. Add skim milk, pat of butter, and horseradish. Mix well.

Brussel Sprouts recipe instructions: Add all ingredients in a bowl and mix gently. Flash sauté.

WHAT TO TOAST WITH

Franciscan Cabernet

UNITY HEALTH FOOD FACTS

NUTRITION FACTS PER SERVING (1/4 RECIPE)
CALORIES: 200
CARBOHYDRATE: 2G
FIBER: 0G
PROTEIN: 25G
FAT: TOTAL: 10G / SATURATED: 4G
CHOLESTEROL: 75MG
SODIUM: 200MG

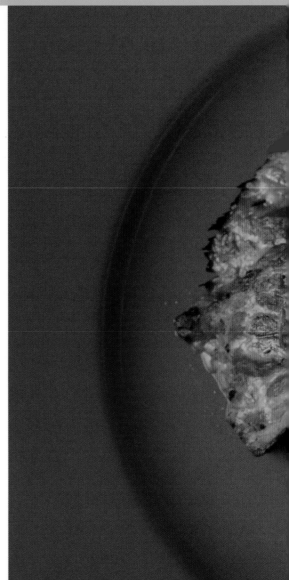

or Sirloin Steak, Sprouts

serves 4-6

Lauren Dixon & Mike Schwabl

CEO AND PRESIDENT, RESPECTIVELY, OF DIXON SCHWABL ADVERTISING

Why is this your favorite healthy entree recipe?
Because of the amount of garlic...we love Grampa Ike's garlic!!

What is your fitness regime?
6am workouts with Kwasi (killer trainer), weight training and stair master and other painful activities.

What is your secret food indulgence?
Lauren: Red licorice. Mike: Ice cream (daily if possible!)

45

NUTRITION FACTS PER SERVING
(1/8 RECIPE)

CALORIES: 330

CARBOHYDRATE: 41G

FIBER: 0G

PROTEIN: 6G

FAT: TOTAL: 16G / SATURATED: 4G

CHOLESTEROL: 160MG

SODIUM: 150MG

Lemon Meringue Pie

Photo Provided

George Eastman

FOUNDER, EASTMAN KODAK COMPANY/ FATHER OF POPULAR PHOTOGRAPHY, LAUNCHED WHAM RADIO IN 1922

Why is this your favorite healthy entrée recipe?

In my day we didn't eat healthy. We didn't know any better. My favorite dinner was homemade fried chicken with pan-fried gravy.

What is your fitness regime?

A horseback ride every morning before breakfast and some citrus every day.

What is your secret food indulgence?

I never start the day without a cup of coffee filled with thick fresh yellow cream!

INGREDIENTS

6 eggs
2 lemons
8 ounces sugar

Crust:
1 cup flour
1/2 cup Crisco® shortening
Pinch of salt
1/2 teaspoon baking powder

WHATCHA GOTTA DO...

Adjust the oven rack to the middle position. Preheat the oven to 375 degrees. Mix crust ingredients and bake crust to a light brown. In a medium bowl, beat yolks of six eggs with sugar. Add juice plus grated rind of two lemons. Cook for 15 minutes in a double boiler, stirring constantly. Take from fire and, when cool, add the beaten whites of three eggs. Fill crust. Make meringue with three remaining egg whites and spoon onto the top of the pie. Put in oven until light brown, about 10-12 minutes at 375 degrees.

Photo Provided

Dr. Dean Edell

1180 WHAM Radio Talk Show Host

Why is this your favorite healthy entrée recipe?

I just love it and it's easy to make. As for health, cooking tomatoes releases cancer-fighting substances called lycopenes. These vitamin-like chemicals are antioxidants that help lower prostate cancer risk. It's a win-win!

What is your fitness regime?

I don't do anything and weigh what I weighed in high school! I do like the outdoors, so I suppose I get some "walking" done there.

What is your secret food indulgence?

Well, it's not at all a secret—everyone knows I'm crazy for coffee!

INGREDIENTS

1½ cup onion, chopped
3 cloves garlic, crushed
4 tablespoon olive oil
4 16 oz. cans Progresso® peeled tomatoes with basil
4 lbs. fresh, ripe plum tomatoes
2 6 oz. cans tomato paste
½ cup red wine vinegar
¼ cup sugar

1 teaspoon dry mustard
2 teaspoon basil
2 teaspoon oregano
2 teaspoon garlic salt
1 teaspoon crushed red pepper
1 teaspoon pepper
2-3 cups water

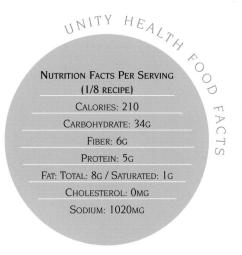

NUTRITION FACTS PER SERVING (1/8 RECIPE)
CALORIES: 210
CARBOHYDRATE: 34G
FIBER: 6G
PROTEIN: 5G
FAT: TOTAL: 8G / SATURATED: 1G
CHOLESTEROL: 0MG
SODIUM: 1020MG

One reason this recipe is so yummy is that it calls for FRESH tomatoes! Add meat, seafood, or vegetables—or enjoy the freshness as is! Dr. Dean's favorite at-home meal is a big salad and spaghetti with marinara and grated pecorino or romano over the top. Tomatoes are very good for you…they're a great source of vitamins A and C, a bunch of minerals, plus lycopene, an antioxidant which is key in the prevention of prostate and all kinds of other cancers. Cooking tomatoes actually releases the lycopenes, so enjoy your pizzas and pastas guilt-free!

Fresh Marinara Sauce serves 8-10

WHATCHA GOTTA DO...

To prepare fresh tomatoes: Place tomatoes in pan of boiling water for a few minutes until the skins split. Drain, cool, and remove skins. They will peel easily. To seed, cut off bottoms and squeeze them. Use a knife to pull out remaining seeds and chop coarsely. In a large Dutch oven, sauté onion and garlic in olive oil for 2-3 minutes. Drain and coarsely chop canned tomatoes, removing seeds the same way you did for the fresh tomatoes. Add all tomatoes (canned and fresh) to onions and garlic. Add all remaining ingredients plus 2 cups of water. Simmer on low heat for 1½ to 2 hours, stirring occasionally. Add water if necessary and more seasonings to taste. The mixture should be thick and most of the water absorbed. Serve over any kind of pasta. This can be made ahead of time, stored in refrigerator, and warmed over medium heat.

WHAT TO TOAST WITH

Ruffino Chianti

Doug Emblidge

13WHAM News Anchor /
Mix 100.5's "Morning Mix with Andrea, Chuck & Doug"

Why is this your favorite healthy entrée recipe?

I ate a lot of salmon to lose some weight last year—
my wife Coleen found this recipe and it helped.

What is your fitness regime?

I'm inconsistent. When I'm in the fitness mode, I like
spinning and the weight circuit at the JCC. In the
summer, I get most of my exercise walking golf
courses. If I'm not hitting the ball straight, these can
be long walks.

What is your secret food indulgence?

It's no secret. I like cookies, but I try to avoid them.

INGREDIENTS

1 *salmon fillet (1½ to 2 lbs.)*
2 *tablespoons cider vinegar*
2 *tablespoons soy sauce*
1 *tablespoon honey*
1 *teaspoon vegetable oil*
1 *teaspoon spicy brown mustard*
⅛ *to ¼ teaspoon ground ginger*
2 *tablespoons sesame seeds, toasted*
3 *green onions, sliced*

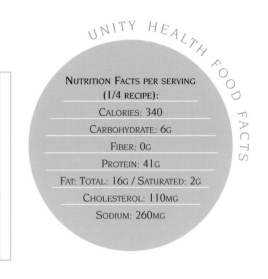

serves 4

Coleen's Sesame Salmon Fillet

WHATCHA GOTTA DO...

Place salmon in a shallow dish. Combine vinegar, soy sauce, honey, oil mustard and ginger—pour over salmon. Cover and refrigerate for 1 hour, turning once. Drain, and discard marinade. Broil the salmon or grill it, covered, over medium-high heat for 15-20 minutes or until the fish flakes easily with a fork. Sprinkle with sesame seeds and onions.

WHAT TO TOAST WITH

Twin Fin
California
Chardonnay

51

Grilled Maple-Glazed Salmon

WE LIKE TO SERVE THIS OVER A BED OF FIELD GREENS ACCOMPANIED WITH A CUCUMBER DILL SALAD AND FOLLOWED BY MARINATED MIXED BERRIES FOR DESSERT.

INGREDIENTS

GLAZED SALMON

2 teaspoons paprika
1 teaspoon chili powder
1 teaspoon ground ancho chile powder
   (can substitute regular chili powder)
½ teaspoon ground cumin
½ teaspoon brown sugar
1 teaspoon sea or kosher salt
4 (6 oz.) salmon fillets (skin removed,
   if desired)
Cooking spray
1-2 teaspoons maple syrup

CUCUMBER DILL SALAD

4 cucumbers, peeled, sliced lengthwise,
   seeded, and cut into thin slices
½ to ¾ cup light sour cream
2 tablespoons fresh chopped dill
1½ teaspoons sea or kosher salt
¼ red onion, very thinly sliced

WHATCHA GOTTA DO...

Pre-heat grill to medium. Combine the first five ingredients (paprika, chili powders, cumin, and brown sugar). Sprinkle fish with salt, then rub with mixed paprika mixture. Place fish on grill rack coated with cooking spray; grill seven minutes. Drizzle fish with syrup. Grill one minute or until fish flakes easily when tested with a fork.

Cucumber Salad—Toss cucumbers with salt and set aside to drain for at least 30 minutes. Squeeze all moisture out of cucumbers. Combine drained cucumbers with remaining ingredients, and then chill until serving time.

serves 6

Nance and Dave Fiedler

ESL FEDERAL CREDIT UNION

Why is this your favorite healthy entrée recipe?
We've become big salmon fans over the last couple of years and we like to grill out year 'round. This fits the bill on both accounts. Plus it is remarkably easy to make!

What is your fitness regime?
Dave: Ride a stationary bike and play golf
Nance: Walk, tennis, tap dance

What is your secret food indulgence?
Dave: Fried dough with cinnamon
Nance: Chocolate of any kind

NUTRITION FACTS PER SERVING
(1/4 SALMON RECIPE)

CALORIES: 250

CARBOHYDRATE: 2G

FIBER: 0G

PROTEIN: 34G

FAT: TOTAL: 11G / SATURATED: 1.5G

CHOLESTEROL: 95MG

SODIUM: 660MG

WHAT TO TOAST WITH

Simi
Sonoma
Chardonnay

Lemon and Herb Roast Chicken w/ Roasted Asparagus

INGREDIENTS

CHICKEN

1 *medium lemon*

2 *tablespoons olive oil*

2 *cloves garlic, minced*

1 *tablespoon minced fresh parsley*
   (stems reserved)

2 *teaspoons minced fresh thyme (stems reserved)*

1/2 *teaspoon minced fresh rosemary*
   (stems reserved)

2 *teaspoon minced fresh sage (stems reserved)*

1/2 *teaspoon salt*

1/2 *teaspoon fresh ground pepper*

1 *whole chicken, 3 to 3 1/2 lb.*

SALAD

1/3 *cup minced shallots (about 2 large)*

2 *tablespoon fresh lemon juice*

2 *tablespoon Sherry wine vinegar*

2 *teaspoon grated lemon peel*

1 1/2 *teaspoon Dijon mustard*

1 *lb. asparagus (tough ends removed)*

6 *cups arugula or mixed field greens*
   (about 5 oz.)

3 *tablespoons chopped fresh chives*

1/2 *cup grated Parmesan cheese*

WHATCHA GOTTA DO...

Finely shred the peel from the lemon, avoiding the white pithy layer (you should have about 1 teaspoon of peel). Remove remaining white layer from lemon. Halve lemon. For herb paste, combine lemon peel, olive oil, garlic, minced herbs, salt, and pepper. Rinse chicken, pat dry. Rub herb paste over chicken. Place reserved herb stems and lemon halves inside. Tie drumsticks together, tuck wing tips under back. Place chicken, breast side down, on a rack in a shallow roasting pan. Roast in 400 degree oven for 30 minutes. Carefully turn the chicken, breast side up, roast for 30 to 35 minutes (180 to 185 degrees on meat thermometer). Remove herb stems and lemon from cavity. Cover chicken loosely with foil. Let stand for 10 minutes before carving. Serve with roasted asparagus salad (recipe follows) if desired.

Salad: While chicken roasts, whisk first 5 ingredients in small bowl to blend. Gradually whisk in olive oil. Season with salt and pepper. Let stand at room temperature. Place asparagus spears on rimmed baking sheet. Drizzle 1/4 cup vinaigrette over and turn to coat, then spread in single layer. Sprinkle with salt and pepper. While chicken rests under foil, roast asparagus at 400 degrees until crisp tender (10 to 12 minutes). Combine arugula, chives, and asparagus in bowl. Add remaining vinaigrette and toss. Sprinkle with salt, pepper, and Parmesan cheese. This salad can be served warm or at room temperature. Cook time: 1 hour

WHAT TO TOAST WITH

Simi
Sonoma
Chardonnay

UNITY HEALTH FOOD FACTS

NUTRITION FACTS PER SERVING
(1/4 RECIPE):

CALORIES: 250

CARBOHYDRATE: 8G

FIBER: 3G

PROTEIN: 13G

FAT: TOTAL: 18G / SATURATED: 6G

CHOLESTEROL: 30MG

SODIUM: 410MG

Jane Flasch

13WHAM NEWS REPORTER

Why is this your favorite healthy entrée recipe?

My mother, Marijane, worked full time while I was growing up but still cooked every night. Even with three active teenagers, dinner served at the family table together was a priority.

I love this recipe because it is a fresh take on the comfort food that we often enjoyed—roast chicken, mashed potatoes and gravy! Herbs from the garden infuse so much flavor you don't even miss the gravy (well almost)!

What is your fitness regime?

I try to get to the gym three times a week (40 minutes of cycling, 20 minutes of weight training) but I admit I often trade workouts for precious time digging in the garden or taking my retriever, Ripley, to the lake for a walk and swim!

What is your secret food indulgence?

German food! Bratwurst cooked in beer (then grilled), Grammy Flasch's German potato salad (with a pound of bacon), Grandma Gosseck's potato pancakes (fried in oil). Not for the timid or the calorie conscious!

Saturday Night Caribbean Julienne Salad

INGREDIENTS

1 'toe' of garlic, smashed to peel & chopped fine

½ teaspoon salt (or less)

1 ½" piece fresh ginger, minced

1 large jalapeño pepper: stem, seed, chopped very fine

2 scallions, with green, chopped fine

¼ cup lime juice

¼ cup brown sugar

1 lb. large shrimp (21-25) raw, cleaned & de-veined

1 tablespoon oil

Salt & pepper

WHATCHA GOTTA DO...

Saturday AM, before it gets hot, cook the shrimp! Mix all sauce ingredients in a small bowl. Pat shrimp dry, season with salt and pepper. Heat oil in a heavy fry pan, almost to smoking hot. Sauté shrimp about 2 minutes until they turn pink. Remove from heat, add 2 tablespoons sauce, toss to coat. Chill shrimp for later, chill sauce (still in the separate dish). Build your favorite salad in a bowl for each person, top with ¼ of the shrimp, serve the remaining sauce for a no-fat, low-salt salad dressing. Remember—it has never touched the raw shrimp! *Tip:* Grating ginger is impossible, it's so fibrous! The easy way to mince ginger: use a sharp knife! Peel it, cut one end off, cut FINE criss cross (1/16 inch) like a tic-tac-toe board. Then slice. Remember watching Grandma cut up vegetables against her thumb? That really works best!

UNITY HEALTH FOOD FACTS

NUTRITION FACTS PER SERVING
(1/4 RECIPE)

CALORIES: 220

CARBOHYDRATE: 19G

FIBER: 2G

PROTEIN: 24G

FAT: TOTAL: 6G / SATURATED: 1G

CHOLESTEROL: 170MG

SODIUM: 480MG

Shrimp

serves 4

Nick & Elaine Francesco (& Amelia!)

1180 WHAM Radio Host, "Sound Bytes"

Why is this your favorite healthy entrée recipe?

We love shrimp in any form, and the sauce is a great tangy/sweet combination, without being too hot. The shrimp alone makes a great appetizer, too! Serve with the sauce for dipping. Elaine collects regional cookbooks to read and to cook from. She discovered that it's an old southern term to refer to a clove of garlic as a 'toe'—what a great image!

What is your fitness regime?

I've lost 35 pounds (and counting!) in just six weeks and I did it using a great diet I've never heard of anywhere else. I call it the ELEM diet, because it's so ELEMentary. That's right—ELEM—Eat Less, Exercise More! How hard is that? It's all about calories in, calories out. Fad diets don't work. This does.

What is your secret food indulgence?

Elaine: Chocolate chip cookies with my first cup of coffee, when only the dogs and I are awake.

Nick: Anything that combines chocolate and peanut butter. A great snack when I'm doing a late-night session on the computer.

INGREDIENTS

2 *beaten eggs*
1 ½ *cups milk*
1 *cup all-purpose flour*
1 *tablespoon cooking oil*
½ *teaspoon sugar (optional)*
1 *teaspoon vanilla (optional)*

NUTRITION FACTS PER SERVING
(1/8 RECIPE WITHOUT FILLINGS)

CALORIES: 50	
CARBOHYDRATE: 6G	
FIBER: 0G	
PROTEIN: 2G	
FAT: TOTAL: 2G / SATURATED: 0.5G	
CHOLESTEROL: 25MG	
SODIUM: 20MG	

WHAT TO TOAST WITH

Heron Hill
Johannisberg
Riesling

serves 6 - 8

Low-Fat Crêpes

WHATCHA GOTTA DO...

Combine eggs, milk, flour, oil, sugar, and vanilla (these last two items are optional). Beat or use blender until well mixed. Heat a lightly greased 6" skillet. Remove from heat. Spoon in 2 to 4 tablespoons of batter. Quickly lift and tilt skillet to spread batter. Return to heat. Brown lightly one side. Gently loosen with spatula and flip to brown the other side. Repeat with remaining batter. Makes approximately 18 crêpes. Fill with your favorite fillings (seafood, fruit, ice cream, etc.) Teddy's favorite "unhealthy" filling is granulated sugar.

Photo Provided

Teddy Geiger

MUSICIAN: CD "UNDERAGE THINKING", COLUMBIA LABEL, TO DEBUT FEBRUARY 2006

Why is this your favorite healthy entrée recipe?

My mom's family is half Spanish and a family favorite is crêpes, but we call them "Spanish Pancakes." We usually eat them with sprinkled sugar or ice cream inside. But they are great with healthy filling choices too! Actually, my dad who has no Spanish in him at all, makes the best crêpes and taught me his "special" technique…it's all in the wrist.

What is your fitness regime?

When I am on the road, playing three to four concerts a week and traveling between shows by van, keeping to a "regime" isn't easy. But performing a concert is quite a workout (and an adrenaline rush)! While on the road, I swim a lot, and the best is when we're near the ocean! I always feel better after a good swim.

What is your secret food indulgence?

Candy (Hot Tamales; hard, sour candy; Lemon Heads; Fireballs!) and caffeine (Starbucks® and Red Bull® are a "pre-concert" must)!

59

Chicken Marsala & Oriental Salad

serves 4

INGREDIENTS

Chicken tenders (1½ to 2 lbs. of chicken)
1 to 1½ cups Marsala cooking wine
2 tablespoons butter

12 oz. fresh mushrooms, sliced
Flour (to dredge chicken)

WHATCHA GOTTA DO...

Dredge chicken tenders in flour, shake off excess. Heat about 2 tablespoons of butter in frying pan and brown cutlets (cooking temperature for the chicken should be 165 degrees). Add more butter as you go. When all browned, add 1 to 1½ cups Marsala cooking wine and immediately cover with pan lid. Add mushrooms and submerge mushrooms to cook. Simmer and add salt and pepper to taste. Once mushrooms are fully cooked, you can serve over mashed potatoes or noodles. While simmering, you can add more butter to make sauce more creamy.

Cook time: Approximately 20 to 30 minutes

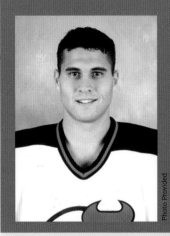

Photo Provided

Brian Gionta

PROFESSIONAL ATHLETE — NEW JERSEY DEVILS

Why is this your favorite healthy entrée recipe?

Anything "chicken" is good with me! It's quick and easy to prepare for a busy lifestyle and it seems as though you prepared it all day. It can be used to entertain or for a quiet night alone.

What is your fitness regime?

With my profession, I have to train regularly. My summer workouts consist of weight and cardio training five times a week. I also have to skate three to four times a week. Off-ice training consists of weights and a lot of running for cardio.

What is your secret food indulgence?

I love Chocolate Better Batter from Maggie Moo's Ice Cream Shop or just plain vanilla ice cream with chocolate sauce.

Blackstone
California
Merlot

UNITY HEALTH FOOD FACTS

NUTRITION FACTS PER SERVING
(1/4 RECIPE)

CALORIES: 420

CARBOHYDRATE: 16G

FIBER: 1G

PROTEIN: 49G

FAT: TOTAL: 8G / SATURATED: 4G

CHOLESTEROL: 130MG

SODIUM: 200MG

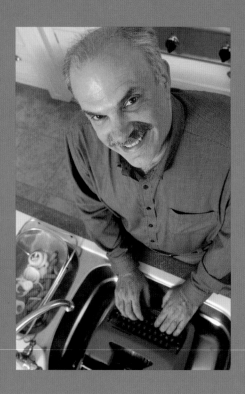

Randy Gorbman

1180 WHAM Radio News Director

Why is this your favorite healthy entrée recipe?

Because it's quick and easy—and I came up with it (more or less).

What is your fitness regime?

I type really, really fast in the newsroom—and I like to walk a lot.

What is your secret food indulgence?

It's no secret…chocolate. Particularly dark chocolate and lots of it!

INGREDIENTS

1 lb. chicken breast, cut into bite-
    sized pieces
1 red pepper, cut into small strips
1 can sliced water chestnuts
1 can sliced mushrooms
Couple of celery stalks, cut into
    small pieces
Couple of garlic cloves, cut up
Powdered ginger
Teaspoon or so tamari or
    soy sauce
Half-teaspoon or so of olive oil
1 cup brown rice

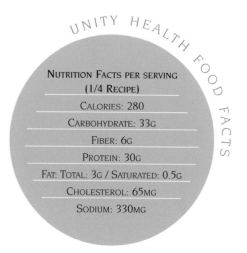

UNITY HEALTH FOOD FACTS

NUTRITION FACTS PER SERVING
(1/4 RECIPE)

CALORIES: 280

CARBOHYDRATE: 33G

FIBER: 6G

PROTEIN: 30G

FAT: TOTAL: 3G / SATURATED: 0.5G

CHOLESTEROL: 65MG

SODIUM: 330MG

Chicken Stir Fry

serves 1-2

WHATCHA GOTTA DO...

Brown chicken over medium-high heat in olive oil wok or non-stick fry pan (if there's too much fat from cooking, take some of it off). Add a little tamari sauce. Add a couple of cloves of garlic, finely chopped (keep stirring the mixture as you go) and add powdered ginger. Add the sliced red pepper, water chestnuts, celery, and sliced mushrooms. Stir well and reduce heat (add more tamari or soy sauce as desired). Simmer (with a cover) for about 10 to 15 minutes. Prepare brown rice according to package directions. Pour chicken mixture over rice, mix well and serve.

Cook time: (including prep work) about a half-hour or less.

WHAT TO TOAST WITH

Simi
Sonoma
Chardonnay

Photo Provided

Elisabeth Hasselbeck

ABC TV's "The View" Co-Host

INGREDIENTS

2 cups Rice Krispies®
2 lbs. crunchy peanut butter
1 lb. confectioner's sugar
1 stick margarine softened

6 oz. chocolate chips
1/3 bar of canning wax

UNITY HEALTH FOOD FACTS

NUTRITION FACTS PER SERVING (1/32 RECIPE)
CALORIES: 260
CARBOHYDRATE: 31G
FIBER: 2G
PROTEIN: 7G
FAT: TOTAL: 14G / SATURATED: 3.5G
CHOLESTEROL: 0MG
SODIUM: 220MG

Buckeyes

WHATCHA GOTTA DO...

Mix first 4 ingredients together and form small balls. Melt the chocolate and wax together on stove—smooth consistency. Dip peanut butter balls and let cool on wax paper. Tastes great just out of freezer.

Summer Spaghetti

serves 6

INGREDIENTS

6 tomatoes, chopped (this is the most important
    ingredient… the fresher the better!)
1 large garlic clove, minced
2 cups fresh basil, chopped
¾-1 cup extra virgin olive oil
1 lb. mozzarella cheese, cut into one-inch cubes
Salt and pepper to taste
Romano or Parmesan cheese for topping
1 lb. good quality spaghetti

WHATCHA GOTTA DO…

Marinate the first six ingredients (tomatoes, garlic,
basil, olive oil, mozzarella, salt and pepper) for at least
an hour (the longer the better). Cook spaghetti *al dente*
and drain. While spaghetti is still hot, add marinated
mixture and toss well. Serve with a great loaf of Italian
bread. There's no better seasonal dinner!

Note: You can reduce the fat content by using only
½ cup of oil and part-skim mozzarella cheese.

WHAT TO TOAST WITH

Simi
Sonoma
Merlot

Dr. Joanne Hessney

DIRECTOR, CRITICAL CARE
MEDICINE—
PARK RIDGE HOSPITAL

Why is this your favorite healthy entrée recipe?

I was never much of a 'fan' of spaghetti despite growing up in Niagara County. I was home from college in Utah one summer when my mom (a fantastic cook) announced we were having 'summer spaghetti' for dinner. Needless to say, I was disappointed, expecting meatballs and a heavy red sauce on a 90 degree day. Since that summer day long ago, this has remained my all-time favorite summer dish especially when served with crusty Italian bread, and ice cold watermelon for dessert!

What is your fitness regime?

Start by 'never say never'…bicycle, jet ski, snowshoe, swim, run (when my feet allow), weights, play softball, etc., etc., etc.

What is your secret food indulgence?

Not so secret….frozen M&M's!

Greek Chicken Roll-Ups and Couscous

INGREDIENTS

4 *chicken breast halves pounded thin*
1 *tablespoon feta cheese*
Sun-dried tomatoes (not in oil)
Baby spinach leaves
Olive oil or Pam® cooking spray for baking dish

WHATCHA GOTTA DO...

Pound out each chicken breast between two sheets of plastic wrap until the pieces are about 1/4 inch thick. Layer each chicken breast with some spinach leaves, a small portion of feta cheese, and sun-dried tomatoes. Roll up each chicken breast, starting from the small side up to the larger end of the breast. Place face down in 9 x 13 baking pan sprayed with Pam® cooking spray or olive oil (you can also put a toothpick into each chicken breast to secure it). Serving size: 1 chicken breast per person with some salad and couscous.

Bake at 375 degrees for 45 minutes (juices should run clear)

WHAT TO TOAST WITH

Estancia
Pinot
Grigio

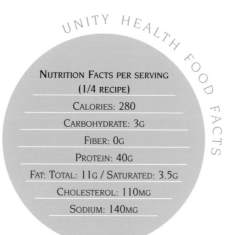

UNITY HEALTH FOOD FACTS

NUTRITION FACTS PER SERVING
(1/4 RECIPE)

CALORIES: 280

CARBOHYDRATE: 3G

FIBER: 0G

PROTEIN: 40G

FAT: TOTAL: 11G / SATURATED: 3.5G

CHOLESTEROL: 110MG

SODIUM: 140MG

Norma Holland

13WHAM News Anchor

Why is this your favorite healthy entrée recipe?

Back in 2001, I traveled to the Greek Islands and to Athens. I remember how good the feta cheese was there, so now I find ways to put it into any dish I can! Also, it's so light and healthy—just like the food in Greece!

What is your fitness regime?

I love to go for walks with my husband. I'm not a power walker, though. I prefer longer, more leisurely strolls. I strive for distance, not time. Also, I try to limit my carbohydrates. Diabetes runs in my family, so I'm very careful about making sure to incorporate some protein into every meal.

What is your secret food indulgence?

I'm Puerto Rican and that means rice and beans, baby! I love a plate of my mother's rice and red beans and some roast pork and fried plantains. It doesn't get any more traditional than that. We usually eat this way for special occasions, such as holidays and family reunions. But sometimes mom makes it "just because" so I make sure I'm there!

NUTRITION FACTS PER SERVING
(1/4 RECIPE):

CALORIES: 630

CARBOHYDRATE: 36G

FIBER: 5G

PROTEIN: 49G

FAT: TOTAL: 33G / SATURATED: 3.5G

CHOLESTEROL: 120MG

SODIUM: 1170MG

WHAT TO TOAST WITH

Heron Hill
Semi-Dry
Riesling

Santa Fe Chicken

serves 4

INGREDIENTS

1 Reynolds® Hot Bags® foil bag,
   large size

4 skinless and boneless chicken
   breasts, cut in large chunks

1 cup Wegmans Santa Fe
   Marinade (regular or fat free)

16 oz. bag frozen corn

2 medium peppers (red, yellow,
   and/or green), cubed or diced

1 medium onion, peeled and
   cut in eighths, or diced

Glenn Johnson (with sons Greg & Matt)

13WHAM-TV/1180 WHAM Radio Chief Meteorologist

Why is this your favorite healthy entrée recipe?

Let it be known that I am not a great chief. Most of my "cooking" is done in the 13 WHAM Forecast Center…but when I do head to the grill, it's usually the BBQ grill. My wife, Eileen, knows this is the place that I can get into the least amount of trouble. She has found that the Santa Fe chicken recipe is largely error free (similar to my weather forecasts). Now I wish I could take most of the credit for this healthy dish, but honestly, I just follow directions very well. However, I do know from experience that this is a delicious meal and is great for the families on the run.

What is your fitness regime?

Over the years, I've tried many work-out routines. This has included the usual fitness centers and gyms. I've participated in golf, softball, and, for quite a long time, I played racquetball. What has worked best for me has been mountain biking. Riding the many trails near the Erie Canal during the spring and summer is a great way to burn calories. This also seems be a little easier on the knees as I "coast" through my 40s. During the long winter months I bring the bike inside and use it as a stationary bike in the basement.

What is your secret food indulgence?

Chocolate-covered cherries by the box. My grandmother treated me to this special dessert as a young boy and I guess I never grew out of it. Although I don't indulge quite as often, now my mother-in-law knows how to soften me up.

WHATCHA GOTTA DO…

Preheat grill to medium high. Pour marinade over chicken; coat well. Transfer chicken and marinade to foil bag. Top with vegetables. Double-fold open end of foil. Place bag on grill rack. Grill, covered, for 30 minutes. Cut open top of bag, wearing oven mitts, and, using a sharp knife, carefully fold back foil, allowing steam to escape. Serve with brown rice, or over cooked corn.

Optional serving suggestion shown in photo: marinated and grilled whole chicken breast.

NUTRITION FACTS PER 1/4 RECIPE
(ABOUT 2 PCS.)

CALORIES: 650

CARBOHYDRATE: 13G

FIBER: 0G

PROTEIN: 37G

FAT: TOTAL: 50G / SATURATED: 12G

CHOLESTEROL: 140MG

SODIUM: 1090MG

WHAT TO TOAST WITH

Franciscan
Cuvée
Sauvage

Photo Provided

Star's Southern Fried Chicken

serves 4

Star Jones Reynolds

ABC TV's "THE VIEW" CO-HOST

INGREDIENTS

One whole chicken cut into 8 pieces
    (2 breasts, 2 wings, 2 thighs,
    2 drumsticks)
Lowry's® seasoning salt
Poultry seasoning
Garlic powder
Salt
Pepper
¼ cup all-purpose flour
¼ cup of Aunt Jemima® pancake mix

Vegetable oil
Deep fryer
Plate lined with paper towels for blotting
    and draining
Tongs for removing chicken
Large Ziploc® bag

WHATCHA GOTTA DO...

Prep time: 30 minutes. Season both sides of chicken with all seasonings. Put in shallow pan, cover with aluminum foil and allow to sit in refrigerator for at least 2 hours so that seasonings will be absorbed into chicken. Pre-heat the vegetable oil to just above medium (1 click past medium on the deep fryer). Oil must be hot, but not scalding. Combine flour and pancake mix in a large Ziploc® bag. Put chicken pieces in bag, close it and shake. Coat the chicken completely and put chicken in fryer. Cook until golden brown. Take chicken out of fryer when brown and put on paper towels to absorb excess oil. Let cool for 5-10 minutes. Enjoy!

Basil pasta "a la Jurs"

INGREDIENTS

1 *ripe seeded tomato
   (remove skin, if desired)*
1 *handful fresh basil leaves*
1 *clove garlic, smallish size*
1 *slice provolone and/or
   mozzarella cheese,
   torn into small pieces*
5 *to 6 ripe olives, halved*
3 *tablespoons olive oil*
1 *serving pasta*

WHATCHA GOTTA DO...

Chop the tomatoes, basil, and garlic into a salsa consistency. Put in a bowl with olive oil, provolone and/or mozzarella cheese, olives, salt, and cracked pepper. Marinate for two minutes or two hours (however long you can wait!) Toss with your favorite pasta, very hot. Serve in handmade ceramic bowls with grated Romano or Parmesan cheese.

WHAT TO TOAST WITH

Nobilo
Marlborough
Sauvignon
Blanc

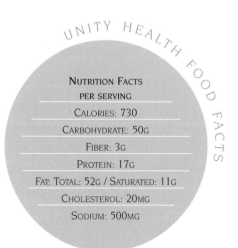

UNITY HEALTH FOOD FACTS

NUTRITION FACTS
PER SERVING
CALORIES: 730
CARBOHYDRATE: 50G
FIBER: 3G
PROTEIN: 17G
FAT: TOTAL: 52G / SATURATED: 11G
CHOLESTEROL: 20MG
SODIUM: 500MG

Nancy Jurs

Artist

Why is this your favorite healthy entrée recipe?

The basil pasta wins all contests for me.

What is your fitness regime?

Lift 50 lb. bags of clay. Haul big sculptures around the garden in 95 degree weather. Drag hundreds of feet of garden hose around. Shovel paths in the snow for my dogs.

What is your secret food indulgence?

Edy's® Espresso Chip ice cream!

INGREDIENTS

2 cups diced potatoes

1 cup (8 oz.) lobster meat (you can substitute crab)

1 cup (8 oz.) small sea scallops

1 cup (8 oz.) shrimp

1 cup minced clams

3½ cups clam juice

4 oz. butter

½ cup flour

¾ cup mirepoix (diced onion, celery, and carrot)

1 cup bottled Bloody Mary mix

2 tablespoons minced garlic

1 tablespoon horseradish (optional)

2½ cups light cream

Salt, as needed

2 teaspoons ground black pepper

3 bay leaves

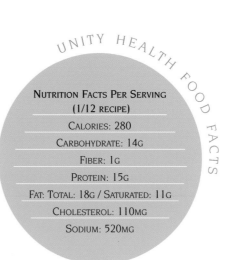

UNITY HEALTH FOOD FACTS

NUTRITION FACTS PER SERVING
(1/12 RECIPE)

CALORIES: 280

CARBOHYDRATE: 14G

FIBER: 1G

PROTEIN: 15G

FAT: TOTAL: 18G / SATURATED: 11G

CHOLESTEROL: 110MG

SODIUM: 520MG

WHAT TO TOAST WITH

Estancia Pinot Grigio

Seafood Chowder

serves 12

WHATCHA GOTTA DO...

Peel and de-vein the shrimp, and cut into bite-sized chunks. Rinse the scallops and clams, drain. Place the clam juice in a stockpot and bring to a boil. Cook the shrimp in the clam juice, then remove and set aside. Do the same thing with the scallops, saving the stock. Cut the lobster meat into bite-sized chunks. Wash the diced tomatoes, drain, and place in the stockpot with the hot clam stock. Bring the potatoes to a boil; add the bay leaves and simmer until the potatoes are tender. In a separate stockpot, melt the butter and sauté the mirepoix and garlic until the onions become transparent. Add the Bloody Mary mix and cook for several minutes. Add the flour to the butter-and-onion mixture to make a roux, and cook over a low heat for several minutes. Add the hot clam stock through a strainer a cup at a time, and whisk until smooth. Add the remaining potatoes and bring to a simmer. Add the light cream, black pepper, and lobster, shrimp and scallops and return to a simmer until heated through. Stir in the horseradish. Adjust the seasoning as desired.

Serve with oyster crackers or hearty grain rolls.

Tom Keller

MORNING ANNOUNCER/ 95.1 THE FOX

Why is this your favorite healthy entrée recipe?

My wife, Maryalice, and I have enjoyed making variations of this recipe. It makes a great cold weather meal, and tastes as good or better for lunch the next day. Since it takes a good hour to prepare, it's a fun, two-person production. We usually enjoy a glass or two of wine in the process.

What is your fitness regime?

Golfing and swimming in the summer; walking our dog, Ranger, often; and a never-ending variety of home-improvement projects!

What is your secret food indulgence?

A bowl of ice cream while watching late-night detective and forensic shows.

Spicy Sesame Noodles with Chicken

serves 4

INGREDIENTS

12 oz. dried or 1 lb. fresh linguine
1 tablespoon sesame seeds
2 tablespoons vegetable oil
8 oz. boneless, skinless chicken breasts,
   thinly sliced
1/3 cup smooth peanut butter
1/2 cup hot water
1 tablespoon soy sauce
1 tablespoon distilled white vinegar
1 tablespoon honey
1 tablespoon oriental sesame oil
1/4 teaspoon dried red pepper flakes
1 green onion, sliced diagonally

WHATCHA GOTTA DO...

In a stockpot, bring 4 quarts of water to boil. Cook linguine in the boiling water according to package directions or until tender but still firm to the bite. Meanwhile, in a large skillet, toast sesame seeds over moderate heat until golden, shaking the pan constantly. Place the seeds in a small bowl and set aside. In the same skillet, heat vegetable oil. Add chicken slices and stir-fry until cooked through, about two to three minutes. Remove the skillet from heat. In a medium-size bowl, blend peanut butter and water. Stir in soy sauce, vinegar, honey, sesame oil, and pepper flakes. Drain the pasta thoroughly and transfer it to a serving bowl. Pour the peanut butter mixture over the linguine and stir until well coated. Toss the linguine with the chicken and its juices. Sprinkle with the toasted sesame seeds and green onion, and serve immediately.

Cook time: 26 minutes

WHAT TO TOAST WITH

Heron Hill
Dry Riesling

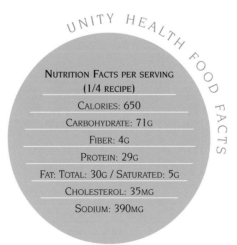

UNITY HEALTH FOOD FACTS

NUTRITION FACTS PER SERVING
(1/4 RECIPE)
CALORIES: 650
CARBOHYDRATE: 71G
FIBER: 4G
PROTEIN: 29G
FAT: TOTAL: 30G / SATURATED: 5G
CHOLESTEROL: 35MG
SODIUM: 390MG

Kathy Kriz

3WHAM NEWS SPECIAL PROJECT REPORTER

Why is this your favorite healthy entrée recipe?

I love this recipe because of the combination of the flavors: the peanut butter, honey, green onion, and sesame seeds. It's like take-out at your favorite Chinese place, without ever having to go out. This is one great option for a cool night when you feel like staying in.

What is your fitness regime?

I'm addicted to Pilates classes. And I use the stationary bike and the elliptical machines at the gym for my cardio workout.

What is your secret food indulgence?

Caramel; I have no resistance to caramel corn. Caramel brownies are my downfall too. So are chewy caramel candies…you get the idea. For Superman, Kryptonite makes him weak…for me, it's caramel!

INGREDIENTS

Sauce:

2 tablespoons olive oil

4 garlic cloves

¼ cup tomato paste

3 cans Italian peeled tomatoes—
   28- to 35- oz. (purée style works
   best—if you can't find, use
   canned tomatoes with no seeds)

2 cups water

Salt and pepper

6 fresh basil leaves, cut small

Meatballs:

1 lb. ground beef (95% lean—you
   may substitute ground turkey)

½ cup plain bread crumbs
   (seasoned may be substituted)

2 large eggs

1 teaspoon minced garlic

½ cup grated Parmigiano-
   Reggiano or Pecorino Romano
   cheese

2 tablespoons flat leaf parsley—
   finely chopped

Salt and pepper

2 tablespoons olive oil

NUTRITION FACTS
(PER MEATBALL)

CALORIES:	130
CARBOHYDRATE:	5G
FIBER:	0G
PROTEIN:	13G
FAT: TOTAL: 7G / SATURATED: 3G	
CHOLESTEROL:	60MG
SODIUM:	400MG

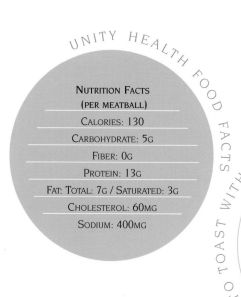

Franciscan
Magnificant

Red Sauce and Meatballs

WHATCHA GOTTA DO...

Sauce: Get started by preparing the tomatoes. If you want a smooth sauce, use a blender to purée the tomatoes. For a chunkier sauce, use canned whole tomatoes and just chop them up in small pieces. Add olive oil to pot and add garlic cloves. Cook on medium to medium-high heat until the garlic is golden. Remove the garlic and discard. Add the tomato paste and stir for about a minute. Now add tomatoes and water. Salt and pepper to taste. Add basil and bring to a simmer. Partially cover the pot and cook over low heat for 2 hours. Stir occasionally. If the sauce starts to get too thick for your taste, just add more water. Once the sauce is on its way, move onto the meatballs.

Meatballs: In a large bowl, combine all the ingredients except oil. Mix together with your hands (the fun part). Rinse your hands with cool water. This will help keep the mixture from sticking to your hands as you roll your meatballs. The meatballs can be whatever size suites your taste. Heat the olive oil in a large skillet and brown the meatballs on all sides. They will finish cooking in the sauce. Put meatballs aside once they're browned. After the sauce has cooked for 2 hours, add the meatballs to the sauce and continue cooking for another 30 to 45 minutes. Serve with your favorite pasta. Freeze the rest to have whenever. Cook time: 2-3 hours, because great tasting food takes time and you need to be able to taste the love. Serving size: just enough to coat your pasta. Remember, noodles can't swim.

Joe Lomonaco—a.k.a. JoeLO

1180 WHAM Production Director,
Host, WHAM 5 O'Clock News Hour

Why is this your favorite healthy entrée recipe?

My grandmother, Theresa Grillo, was an amazing cook. I spent a great deal of time in her kitchen when I was growing up and I love the look of satisfaction she got from feeding people. A lot of what she put on the table came from her own garden, right down to the tomatoes in the homemade sauce. So, every time I make this sauce myself, I think of grandma. Just the smell of it brings me back to her kitchen on Delmar Street in Binghamton, New York. I don't grow my own tomatoes, but when I get to see people enjoying a meal I've made for them, I get the same satisfaction. And, in my mind's eye, I get a little smile from grandma.

What is your fitness regime?

I'm a big fan of walking. And since my wife and I are proud parents of a young border terrier named Cooper, we do a ton of walking around our neighborhood. You can put in a few miles a day easily when you're on the other end of the leash. And the best part is you don't ever realize you're exercising. You're just out having fun with the dog. How cool is that?

What is your secret food indulgence?

I am a sucker for peanut butter. You can put peanut butter on anything and I'll eat it. No really. Try me. An old shoe? Sure, just put some peanut butter on it. Snow tire? Yep, fill it with peanut butter. Do I eat it straight out of the jar? You bet. Do I put it on ice cream? Oh, yes.

81

INGREDIENTS

Recipe Ingredients for Chicken Chalupas:

1 dozen flour tortillas
4 large chicken breasts, boiled and diced
2 cans cream of chicken soup
1 pint sour cream
½ lb. grated Monterey Jack or Pepper Jack cheese
¾ lb. grated cheddar cheese
½ bunch green onions and tops
1 small can sliced olives
1 small can green chili peppers (optional)

Recipe Ingredients for Taffy Apple Salad:

6-8 Granny Smith apples
8 oz. package Cool Whip®
½ cup crushed peanuts
1 can crushed pineapple with syrup
1 tablespoon flour
1 egg, beaten
½ cup sugar

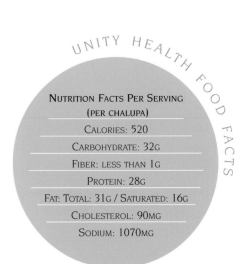

UNITY HEALTH FOOD FACTS

NUTRITION FACTS PER SERVING
(PER CHALUPA)

CALORIES: 520

CARBOHYDRATE: 32G

FIBER: LESS THAN 1G

PROTEIN: 28G

FAT: TOTAL: 31G / SATURATED: 16G

CHOLESTEROL: 90MG

SODIUM: 1070MG

Chicken Chalupas and Taffy Apple Salad

WHATCHA GOTTA DO...

Recipe Instructions for Chicken Chalupas: Combine soup, chili peppers, olives, sour cream, and onions. Fold in Monterey Jack cheese. Take two cups of that mixture out. Add diced chicken to remaining mixture. Roll up chicken mixture in tortillas and lay in greased pan. Pour two-cup mixture over top and cover with cheddar cheese. Bake at 350 degrees for 40 minutes.

Bob Lonsberry

1180 WHAM Radio Talk Show Host

**Why is this your favorite healthy
entrée recipe?**

I don't know that it's particularly healthy, but
it's tasty and my wife enjoys making it. The
most important part of good health is peace
of mind, and the food you enjoy prepared by
someone you love is great peace of mind.

What is your fitness regime?

I run 9 to 12 miles, five to six times a week. I
also bike and hike.

What is your secret food indulgence?

It's no secret—I enjoy anything involving the
word "buffet."

Baked Chicken Breasts and Rice

serves 2 hungry people

INGREDIENTS

2 boneless, skinless chicken breasts
½ cup uncooked rice
¼ cup red & green peppers, chopped
⅛ cup sun-dried tomatoes, chopped
⅛ cup artichoke hearts, chopped
⅛ cup onions, chopped
Basil and tarragon
1 cup white wine
¼ cup water
Salt & pepper to taste

WHATCHA GOTTA DO...

Combine all ingredients except chicken and rice in an 8-inch glass baking dish. Pre-heat oven to 400 degrees. Place chicken in dish, trying to trap as little of the veggies beneath it as possible. Add rice and spread it throughout the liquid, taking care not to get rice atop the exposed portions of the chicken breasts. Cook time: 25 minutes at 400 degrees or until rice is cooked. Baste chicken with liquid, from time to time, during cooking.

Cook time: 25 minutes

Bill Lowe

1180 WHAM RADIO
MORNING NEWS ANCHOR

Why is this your favorite healthy entrée recipe?

Chicken, walnuts, and green peppers made in the wok.

What is your fitness regime?

Three days a week at the gym on the treadmill, rowing machine, and elliptical machine. Also, at least one day a week of yard work around the house.

What is your secret food indulgence?

Ice cream...darn near any flavor.

WHAT TO TOAST WITH

Nobilo
Marlborough
Sauvignon
Blanc

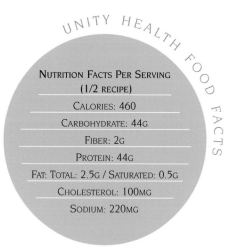

UNITY HEALTH FOOD FACTS

NUTRITION FACTS PER SERVING
(1/2 RECIPE)

CALORIES: 460

CARBOHYDRATE: 44G

FIBER: 2G

PROTEIN: 44G

FAT: TOTAL: 2.5G / SATURATED: 0.5G

CHOLESTEROL: 100MG

SODIUM: 220MG

NUTRITION FACTS PER SERVING
(1/4 RECIPE)

CALORIES: 710

CARBOHYDRATE: 114G

FIBER: 11G

PROTEIN: 24G

FAT: TOTAL: 15G / SATURATED: 2G

CHOLESTEROL: 10MG

SODIUM: 880MG

WHAT TO TOAST WITH

Franciscan
Cuvée
Sauvage

Gap & Janet Mangione

MUSICIAN

Why is this your favorite healthy entrée recipe?

Pasta and beans have been staples of our family for generations. This is an easy and healthy recipe.

What is your fitness regime?

Mostly treadmill and bicycle 2 to 3 times per week at the "Y" for exercise groups.

What is your secret food indulgence?

Not so secret…pasta! I could do that every day at least once.

White Bean and Roasted Chicken Salad

serves 5

INGREDIENTS

Salad Recipe Ingredients:

2 cups coarsely chopped roasted skinless, boneless chicken (about 2 breasts)
1 cup chopped tomato
1/2 cup thinly sliced red onion
1/3 cup sliced fresh basil
2 16 oz. cans cannellini beans or other white beans (kidney or Great Northern), rinsed and drained

Salad Dressing Ingredients:

1/4 cup red wine vinegar
2 tablespoons extra virgin olive oil
1 tablespoon fresh lemon juice
2 teaspoons Dijon mustard
1/2 teaspoon salt
1/4 teaspoon fresh ground pepper
2 cloves garlic, minced

WHATCHA GOTTA DO…

Salad recipe instructions: Place the first five ingredients (coarsely chopped chicken, tomato, onion, basil, and beans) in a large bowl. Stir gently to combine. This is a nutritious, easy, refreshing summer entrée. For winter, add 1/2 lb. pasta shells.

Salad dressing recipe instructions: Combine vinegar and remaining ingredients, stirring with a whisk. Drizzle over salad.

INGREDIENTS

6 boneless chicken breasts (slightly flattened)
Salt and freshly ground pepper to taste
Olive oil
1 bunch fresh sage
1 cup orange juice
2 navel oranges, thinly sliced
4 teaspoons orange marmalade

WHAT TO TOAST WITH

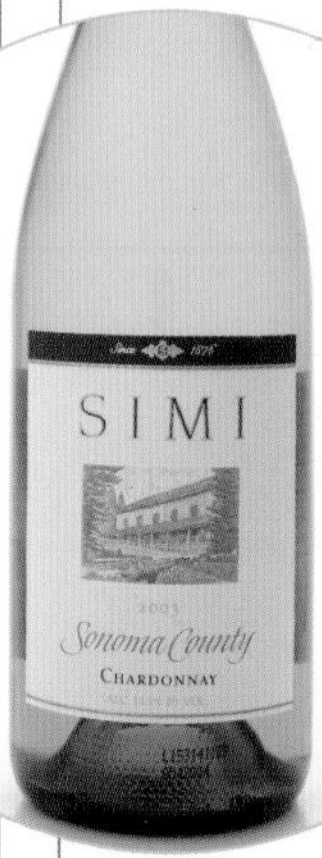

Simi
Sonoma
Chardonnay

SIMI
Sonoma County
CHARDONNAY

serves 4-6

Chicken with Orange and Sage

WHATCHA GOTTA DO...

Preheat oven to 375. Trim excess fat off from chicken, rinse and dry. Sprinkle with salt and pepper. Place on lightly oiled baking pan. Place sage leaf under and on top of each piece of chicken. Drizzle with orange juice. Place a sheet of oiled wax paper directly on chicken. Bake for 10-12 minutes or until cooked through. Cool in the pan. Pour pan juices into saucepan. Reduce, then stir in marmalade. Cook until thickened. Slice the chicken and arrange on platter, alternating with sliced oranges. Spoon the sauce over the chicken. Serve hot for dinner or cold for a luncheon.

Dan Mason

GENERAL MANAGER, ROCHESTER RED WINGS

Why is this your favorite healthy entrée recipe?

I'm very lucky that my wife is an outstanding cook and this is her favorite healthy entrée.

What is your fitness regime?

I walk around the ballpark quite a bit because of my job. I also have two young kids (Cam, 6, and Anna, 4) and they keep me on the run.

What is your secret food indulgence?

I love nachos and cheese. And, if I really want to indulge, I get an order of barbecue pork nachos at the ballpark. They're unreal!

Macaroni and Cheese

Bob Matthews

1180 WHAM RADIO
SPORTS TALK HOST

Why is this your favorite healthy entrée recipe?
This is something my Mom made.

What is your fitness regime?
Walking to the fridge in between innings of a ballgame.

What is your secret food indulgence?
Triple scoop of ice cream from Meisenzahl's Dairy.

INGREDIENTS

1 *package elbow macaroni*
1 *lb. Velveeta® cheese*
1 *cup bread crumbs*
⅓ *cup butter*
¼ *cup milk*

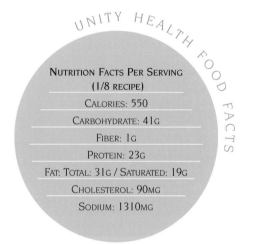

UNITY HEALTH FOOD FACTS

NUTRITION FACTS PER SERVING
(1/8 RECIPE)

CALORIES: 550

CARBOHYDRATE: 41G

FIBER: 1G

PROTEIN: 23G

FAT: TOTAL: 31G / SATURATED: 19G

CHOLESTEROL: 90MG

SODIUM: 1310MG

WHATCHA GOTTA DO...

Cook elbow macaroni according to package directions, then drain. Cut cheese into small chunks. Turn heat down low. Combine milk, butter, and cheese. Simmer until bubbly. Set oven at 350 degrees. Pour into baking dish. Sprinkle bread crumbs on top. Bake until golden brown.

WHAT TO TOAST WITH

Twin Fin California Chardonnay

Franciscan
Cuvée
Sauvage

Garlic-Buttered Shrimp

serves 4

Holly Maynard

13WHAM NEWS REPORTER

INGREDIENTS

1 lb. fresh or frozen peeled and de-
    veined medium-to-large shrimp
¼ cup margarine or butter
1 clove garlic, minced
1 tablespoon snipped fresh parsley
Dash of ground red pepper
3 tablespoons dry white wine
Shredded lettuce (optional)

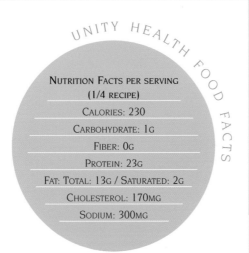

UNITY HEALTH FOOD FACTS

NUTRITION FACTS PER SERVING
(1/4 RECIPE)

CALORIES:	230
CARBOHYDRATE:	1G
FIBER:	0G
PROTEIN:	23G
FAT: TOTAL: 13G / SATURATED: 2G	
CHOLESTEROL:	170MG
SODIUM:	300MG

WHATCHA GOTTA DO...

Thaw shrimp if frozen. For sauce, melt margarine or butter in small saucepan. Stir in garlic, parsley, and red pepper. Cook for 1 minute. Stir in wine; heat through. Set aside. Thread shrimp into 4 long or 8 short skewers. Grill on the greased rack of an uncovered grill directly over medium coals for 6 to 10 minutes or until shrimp are opaque on the inside. Turn once halfway through grilling time and brush frequently with sauce. Serve on a bed of shredded lettuce, if desired.

Cook time: 6 to 10 minutes

Why is this your favorite healthy entrée recipe?

This recipe reminds me of New England where I grew up. I lived in Connecticut, not too far from the shoreline where the seafood was so good. My mom would make this dish in the summer.

What is your fitness regime?

Sometimes it's hard for me to stay motivated, so I try to vary my workouts. I combine running and weightlifting with kickboxing, cycling, step, yoga, and Pilates classes. The variety helps me look forward to working out, rather than dreading the same old thing. That's key, because I love to find reasons NOT to exercise! I try to work out five to six days a week.

What is your secret food indulgence?

No question—peanut butter pie! I have a hard time resisting it if it's on the dessert menu at restaurants.

Richard McCollough

13WHAM-TV/1180 WHAM Radio Meteorologist

Why is this your favorite healthy entrée recipe?

I like drinking coffee in the morning and, on occasion, I love to have coffee cake. I've shared this special cake with family and friends.

What is your fitness regime?

I have my own small gym at home and do the treadmill and free weights. I drink plenty of water and literally run up my many steps at home every day. I watch what I eat and try to balance workouts with my busy schedule.

What is your secret food indulgence?

It would have to be raspberry ice cream in the summer and chocolate cake in the winter.

INGREDIENTS

Topping:
½ cup walnuts or pecans
½ cup sugar
1 tablespoon ground cinnamon

Batter:
½ cup butter, cut in 4 or more
    pieces

1 cup sugar
1 teaspoon pure vanilla extract
2 eggs
1 cup sour cream
1 ½ cup unsifted all-purpose flour
1 ½ teaspoons baking powder
1 teaspoon baking soda
⅛ teaspoon salt

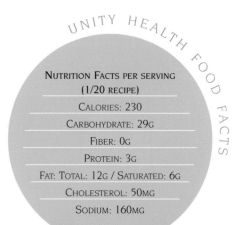

Cinnamon Walnut Coffee Cake

WHATCHA GOTTA DO...

Making the topping: With metal blade in place, add walnuts, ½ cup sugar, and cinnamon to food processor bowl. Process, turning on and off, until mixture is combined and nuts are coarsely chopped. Put mixture onto sheet of waxed paper. Making the batter: Again using blade, add butter, 1 cup sugar, and vanilla to bowl and process until combined, about 30 seconds. Add eggs and sour cream. Process until thoroughly mixed. Combine flour, baking powder, baking soda, and salt. Stir to mix, then add to butter mixture. Turn on and off 3 or 4 times until flour disappears. Grease and flour a 7-9 cup tube pan (an 8-inch springform pan will work too). Place half of batter in pan and top with half cinnamon mixture. Add remaining batter and sprinkle top evenly with remaining cinnamon mixture. Bake in a preheated 350 degree oven for 45-50 minutes. Cool for 10 minutes in pan, turn out rack, turning again so topping side is up, to cool completely.

Tim McCormick

PRESIDENT AND CHIEF EXECUTIVE OFFICER—
UNITY HEALTH SYSTEM

Why is this your favorite healthy entrée recipe?

Great meal—quick and easy to prepare, good with a glass of red wine. Joan and I shared many a night with this simple but delicious meal.

What is your fitness regime?

Swimming, golf, and walking.

What is your secret food indulgence?

Peanut butter.

INGREDIENTS

½ lb. shrimp, fresh or frozen
2 garlic gloves, minced or pressed
2 tablespoons olive oil
1 cup tomatoes, diced
½ cup crumbled feta cheese
Juice ½ lemon
2 teaspoons chopped fresh dill (¾ teaspoon dried)
Dash of salt and ground black pepper

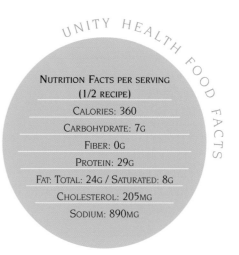

UNITY HEALTH FOOD FACTS

NUTRITION FACTS PER SERVING (1/2 RECIPE)
CALORIES: 360
CARBOHYDRATE: 7G
FIBER: 0G
PROTEIN: 29G
FAT: TOTAL: 24G / SATURATED: 8G
CHOLESTEROL: 205MG
SODIUM: 890MG

Shrimp Feta serves 2

WHATCHA GOTTA DO...

Have all the ingredients prepared and at hand before beginning to sauté. Sauté the garlic in the oil briefly, then add the shrimp. Cook on medium heat for one minute. Add the tomatoes, feta, lemon juice, and dill. Stir so that the shrimp cooks on both sides. When the shrimp are pink and the tomatoes and feta have made a sauce, it's ready. Sprinkle with salt and pepper to taste. Serve at once over rice or pasta with steamed broccoli.

Cook time: 20 minutes total

WHAT TO TOAST WITH

Simi
Sonoma
Chardonnay

97

INGREDIENTS

2 16 oz. cans tomato sauce
1 lb. of lean ground beef
1 lb. hot Italian sausage
2 packages of chili seasoning
2 teaspoons ground cumin
2 teaspoons chili powder
1 tablespoon cumin seed
1 teaspoon cinnamon
1 large Spanish onion
2 small jalapeño peppers
2 cans hot chili beans
2 cans red kidney beans

suggested Sides:

grated cheddar

sour cream

bread bowl

Tostitos®

UNITY HEALTH FOOD FACTS

NUTRITION FACTS PER SERVING
(1/15 RECIPE)

CALORIES: 260

CARBOHYDRATE: 26G

FIBER: 7G

PROTEIN: 18G

FAT: TOTAL: 11G / SATURATED: 4G

CHOLESTEROL: 35MG

SODIUM: 1050MG

WHAT TO TOAST WITH

Simi
Sonoma
Merlot

Slow Cooked Chili serves 15~20

WHATCHA GOTTA DO...

Brown the meat in a large pot. Add onions, peppers, and one packet of chili seasoning while beef is browning. Once beef is browned, drain grease, add tomato sauce, both cans chili beans, and sauce from can. Drain kidney beans, then add to chili and add remaining spices. Bring to boil then cook over low heat, stirring occasionally.

Cook time: 4 hours or so

Mark McLean

13WHAM-TV/1180 WHAM Radio
Meteorologist/Director of Weather
Services

Why is this your favorite healthy entrée recipe?

It's a Superbowl and all-occasions specialty. It's a recipe from a good friend.

What is your fitness regime?

I'm always on the move and working outside in the yard. Landscaping and yard cleanup is my real "second full-time job."

What is your secret food indulgence?

Anything on the menu at Jim and Ralph's Restaurant in Gates. Those guys just know how to grill!

Spicy Honey Salmon Salad and Apple Cake

Kristen Miranda

13WHAM NEWS ANCHOR

Why is this your favorite healthy entrée recipe?

I've only recently started to enjoy salmon, but now I would eat it every day if I could! I really like a salad as an entrée as long as it contains some protein (usually fish or chicken) and lots of crunchy bits so I feel like I'm actually eating something. That's why I like to add the cashews and Craisins®. As for the goat cheese, that's just a rich, fun indulgence.

What is your fitness regime?

I work out six days a week: four days doing cardio at my gym, and two days working with a personal trainer. I also try very hard to get eight hours of sleep each night and drink lots of water. Nobody is perfect—we all slip up on our diet/exercise regime—but I find when I make good food and workout choices, I feel better about myself.

What is your secret food indulgence?

Having said that, I love peanut butter and anything chocolate. If it includes both peanut butter AND chocolate—I'm done for. I also love a big bowl of pasta now and again. Even though my mom's apple cake may sound healthy, it isn't…but I've included the recipe anyway.

INGREDIENTS

Spicy Honey Salmon
4 (6 oz.) pieces of salmon, Cajun seasoning, honey
6 cups mixed field greens (prepackaged)
Plum tomatoes (to taste)
Cucumber (to taste)
Red onion (to taste)
1/3 cup honey roasted cashews
1/3 cup Craisins®
1/3 cup dried pineapple
Crumbled goat cheese (to taste)
Balsamic vinaigrette

Apple Cake
5-6 diced apples
1 cup vegetable oil
1 1/2 cup of sugar
3 eggs
2 1/4 cups flour
1 teaspoon baking soda
1 teaspoon cinnamon
1/2 teaspoon cloves
1/2 teaspoon nutmeg
1 teaspoon salt
1 teaspoon vanilla

WHATCHA GOTTA DO...

Spicy Salmon: Preheat oven to 425. Place salmon steaks on an aluminum-foil-covered baking pan. Coat top of each steak with thin layer of Cajun seasoning. Drizzle moderately with honey. Bake at 425 degrees for 8-10 minutes or until fish is opaque in the center. While fish is baking, combine greens, sliced tomatoes, cashews, Craisins®, red onion, cucumber, and dried pineapple in a large salad bowl. Toss with Balsamic vinaigrette. Divide into four dishes—top each with salmon steak and sprinkle with goat cheese.

Cook time: 8-10 minutes

NUTRITION FACTS PER SERVING
(1/4 SALMON RECIPE)

CALORIES: 650

CARBOHYDRATE: 47G

FIBER: 4G

PROTEIN 44G

FAT: TOTAL: 32G / SATURATED: 8G

CHOLESTEROL: 110MG

SODIUM: 1090MG

Apple Cake: Preheat oven to 350 degrees. Mix together 1 cup vegetable oil, $1\frac{1}{2}$ cups of sugar and 3 eggs and let sit while cutting up apples. Add $2\frac{1}{4}$ cups flour, 1 teaspoon baking soda, 1 teaspoon cinnamon, $\frac{1}{2}$ teaspoon each of cloves and nutmeg, 1 teaspoon salt and 1 teaspoon vanilla. Stir in 5-6 diced apples. Optional $\frac{1}{2}$ to $\frac{3}{4}$ cup of nuts. Pour all ingredients into a well-greased 13 x 9 pan (glass pan is best). Top with cinnamon-sugar mixture. Bake for 45-50 minutes at 350 degrees until toothpick comes out clean.

Brendan O'Riordan

1180 WHAM RADIO,
NEWS REPORTER/ANCHOR

Why is this your favorite healthy entrée recipe?

I learned to cook this at a young age, and that's a feat in itself.

What is your fitness regime?

Thank goodness for the 7th inning stretch and the two minute warning!

What is your secret food indulgence?

Mint Chocolate Chip Ice Cream.

INGREDIENTS

1 large onion, chopped
1 tablespoon butter
4 cups chicken broth
1 head cauliflower, cut up
1 carrot, peeled
1 cup low-fat milk
¼ teaspoon nutmeg
⅛ teaspoon cayenne pepper
Cheddar cheese, shredded

NUTRITION FACTS PER SERVING
(2 TRUFFLES)
CALORIES: 110
CARBOHYDRATE: 11G
FIBER: 3G
PROTEIN: 5G
FAT: TOTAL: 6G / SATURATED: 3G
CHOLESTEROL: 15MG
SODIUM: 760MG

serves 4-6

Cream of Cauliflower Soup

WHATCHA GOTTA DO...

In medium saucepan, sauté onion and butter for 3 minutes. Add broth, cauliflower, and carrot and bring to a boil. Reduce heat, cover, and simmer for 15 minutes. Remove soup from heat and let it cool down until warm. Transfer soup in batches to blender. Add milk and purée until smooth (or use a stick blender). Transfer back to pot and heat gently. Garnish with a pinch of shredded cheddar cheese. Serve with dark pumpernickel bread and a side salad for a perfect light fall meal.

Cook time: 30 minutes

WHAT TO TOAST WITH

Franciscan
Cuvée
Sauvage

Bill Peterson

RETIRED 13WHAM CHIEF METEOROLOGIST

Why is this your favorite healthy entrée recipe?

This was a dish a good friend made for me after my first heart surgery.

What is your fitness regime?

Right now, walking is the extent of my fitness regime—that and getting out of bed everyday.

What is your secret food indulgence?

If beer does not count as a food, then I would have to say fudge is my big indulgence.

INGREDIENTS

⅓ cup chopped onion
1 cup rice
2½ lbs. chicken (cut up)
10½ oz. can of cream of mushroom
  soup
½ can water
¼ teaspoon crushed marjoram
½ teaspoon salt
¼ teaspoon crushed thyme
⅛ teaspoon pepper
⅛ teaspoon oregano
¼ teaspoon chopped parsley

UNITY HEALTH FOOD FACTS

NUTRITION FACTS PER SERVING (1/4 RECIPE)	
CALORIES: 610	
CARBOHYDRATE: 44G	
FIBER: 1G	
PROTEIN: 48G	
FAT: TOTAL: 25G / SATURATED: 7G	
CHOLESTEROL: 155MG	
SODIUM: 950MG	

Chicken with Herbs   serves 4

WHATCHA GOTTA DO...

Lightly grease shallow baking dish which has a tight cover. Sprinkle onion over bottom of dish. Sprinkle rice over the onion. Lay chicken on top of rice—skin side up—careful to not overlap. Combine soup, water, and spices (except parsley). Spoon over chicken and top with parsley. Bake (covered) at 350 degrees for 60 minutes or until chicken is tender. If desired, remove cover last 15 minutes to brown.

WHAT TO TOAST WITH

Simi
Sonoma
Merlot

Chicken and Rice

serves 4

INGREDIENTS

Good Seasons salad dressing*
4 boneless chicken breasts
Rice
Chicken boullion
16 oz. frozen vegetables (broccoli,
    cauliflower, carrots)
Garlic/onion seasoning

*Needs oil and vinegar; follow package
    directions

WHATCHA GOTTA DO...

Preheat oven to 400 degrees. Put chicken breasts in a 9 x 13 dish. Pour Good Seasons dressing on chicken. Bake 20 minutes at 400 degrees. Remove from oven after 20 minutes. Add $^2/_3$ cup rice (sprinkle around chicken) and $1^3/_4$ cup of chicken boullion. Sprinkle onion seasoning and garlic seasoning on chicken. Add 16 oz. bag of vegetables. Put back in oven for 25-30 minutes at 400 degrees (leave uncovered).

Cook time: 45-50 minutes

WHAT TO TOAST WITH

Heron Hill
Dry Riesling

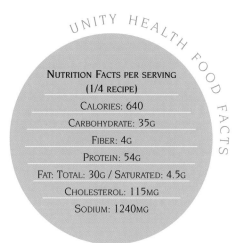

UNITY HEALTH FOOD FACTS

NUTRITION FACTS PER SERVING
(1/4 RECIPE)

CALORIES: 640

CARBOHYDRATE: 35G

FIBER: 4G

PROTEIN: 54G

FAT: TOTAL: 30G / SATURATED: 4.5G

CHOLESTEROL: 115MG

SODIUM: 1240MG

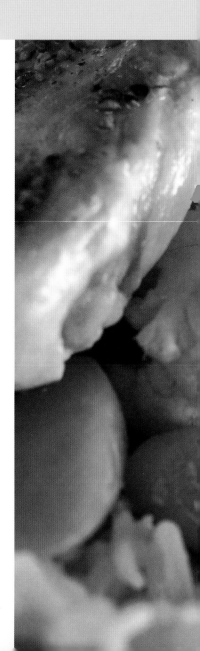

Kevin Roche

13WHAM Sports Anchor

Why is this your favorite healthy entrée recipe?

It's honestly the only thing I really know how to make and, when I do make it, I can eat it all week until it's gone. I love it! Ask anyone that knows me and they'll tell you that I'm always having chicken and rice for dinner.

What is your fitness regime?

I like to run regularly, especially in the summer months here in Rochester. I usually run 4-5 miles a day or more. I'm certainly not a gym rat, but you can find me there from time to time as well.

What is your secret food indulgence?

Sweets!!! Like most people, I love sweets and since I was a little kid I've loved Half Moon cookies (black-and-white cookies). My mom still sends them to me.

Ginny Ryan

13WHAM News Anchor

Why is this your favorite healthy entrée recipe?

It's hard to find a dish that everyone in the family will eat, but this one fits the bill. Better yet—it works well with our busy nights because it's easy to make. We usually have it with couscous and a vegetable.

What is your fitness regime?

I run 2½ miles three to five times a week, depending on my schedule. I'm looking forward to learning Pilates!

What is your secret food indulgence?

Chocolate!

Chicken Breast Scampi

serves 4

INGREDIENTS

1 to 1½ lbs. chicken tenders
⅓ margarine
2-3 garlic gloves
1 tablespoon parsley
1 teaspoon dried dill weed
¼ teaspoon oregano
½ teaspoon salt
½ teaspoon pepper

WHATCHA GOTTA DO...

Melt margarine in saucepan over low heat; add garlic, parsley, dill weed, oregano, salt, and pepper. Cook for two minutes. Place chicken in baking dish; pour margarine mixture over it. Oven temp: 350 degrees.

Cook time: Bake for 10 minutes, turn chicken over and bake for 10 more minutes. Turn again and broil for 2 minutes until lightly browned.

WHAT TO TOAST WITH

Nobilo
Marlborough
Sauvignon
Blanc

Low-Fat Clams Casino on the Half Shell

serves 2

INGREDIENTS

1 *dozen very fresh littleneck clams*
1 *red sweet pepper*
1 *green sweet pepper*
1 *fresh, firm Vidalia onion*
Low-fat imitation bacon bits

WHAT TO TOAST WITH

Estancia
Pinot
Grigio

UNITY HEALTH FOOD FACTS

NUTRITION FACTS PER SERVING
(1/2 RECIPE)

CALORIES: 280

CARBOHYDRATE: 32G

FIBER: 8G

PROTEIN: 23G

FAT: TOTAL: 9G / SATURATED: 1.5G

CHOLESTEROL: 30MG

SODIUM: 560MG

WHATCHA GOTTA DO...

Scrub and wash the clams thoroughly. Make sure all of the clams are tightly closed and very fresh before you begin. Using your favorite clean knife (we have used the same clam knife since 1954), carefully open each clam, removing one half of the shell. Gently loosen the clam from the remaining shell by carefully scraping underneath. Make sure you do not spill or remove the natural clam juices. Set the open half shell—with the clam inside—on a broiler pan. Repeat with all 12 clams. Chop the green and red sweet peppers into 1/4" pieces and place several of each color on top of the clam in each half shell. Chop the Vidalia onion and place a generous amount on top of the peppers. Lastly, sprinkle the imitation bacon bits on top of the entire creation. Using real chopped bacon is an option, but cut away the fat, using only the meaty part of the bacon. Place the clams in a cold oven on broil. Broil the clams for ten minutes turning 90° once. Check often to prevent burning. Remove from the oven and eat at once before they get cold! Optional garnishes include Parmesan cheese, various hot sauces, and fresh ground black pepper. Oven temperature: broiler on high.

Cook time: About 10 minutes, broiling on the lower rack.
Check often, taking care not to burn the tops.

Jim Salmon

1180 WHAM Radio Co-Host, WHAM Home Repair Clinic
President of Jim Salmon Home Inspectors Inc., President of JimSalmon.com

Why is this your favorite healthy entrée recipe?

Healthy eating to me is low-fat, low-cholesterol, and low-carbohydrate. This recipe for clams casino has been in my family for 50 years. My earliest memories of life at the cottage include bags and bags of fresh clams, steamed, casino, and raw. While I have cleaned it up a bit by removing the drawn butter and bacon, this recipe is among the finest foods I have ever eaten. Eating healthy means you can still enjoy a lifelong favorite recipe without feeling guilty—as long as you modernize it slightly. The only problem with this recipe is the clams are eaten as fast as you can make them. It takes me about 30 minutes to shuck 100 clams so plan on spending some quality time with good friends to fully enjoy this creation. Each dozen of littleneck clams has about 100 calories and virtually no measurable fat and with zero carbohydrates.

What is your fitness regime?

My job keeps me very busy running up and down stairs while doing home inspections. My mouth gets a heavy workout each weekend while broadcasting on WHAM. And I always have a home repair project to keep me fit and trim. I eat very few carbohydrates and no sugar. I like camping, water and snow skiing with my kids, and hiking.

What is your secret food indulgence?

Dark beer, elderberry pie, and eggs and bacon cooked over a campfire.

Spaghetti Puttanesca

INGREDIENTS

1 *box spaghetti*
Olive oil
2 *28 oz. cans crushed tomatoes*
Small jar capers
4 *anchovies*
1 *cup white wine*
2 *to 3 cloves of garlic*
10 *green olives, sliced*
Salt and pepper

WHATCHA GOTTA DO...

Prepare spaghetti *al dente*; reserve on side.
Sauté garlic and anchovies in olive oil.
Add crushed tomatoes, capers, wine, and
green olives. Simmer for 30 minutes. Add
salt and pepper to taste. Add spaghetti and
serve immediately.

Cook time: 40 minutes

WHAT TO TOAST WITH

Opus One

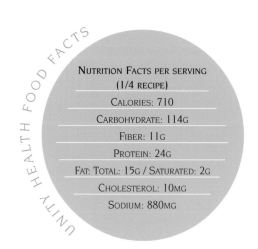

UNITY HEALTH FOOD FACTS

**NUTRITION FACTS PER SERVING
(1/4 RECIPE)**

CALORIES: 710

CARBOHYDRATE: 114G

FIBER: 11G

PROTEIN: 24G

FAT: TOTAL: 15G / SATURATED: 2G

CHOLESTEROL: 10MG

SODIUM: 880MG

Robert Sands

PRESIDENT & COO, CONSTELLATION BRANDS, INC.

Why is this your favorite healthy entrée recipe?

This recipe is a favorite of mine because I love pasta and Italian cuisine.

What is your fitness regime?

Weight training three times a week. Also biking or running 3 times a week, weather permitting.

What is your secret food indulgence?

Toblerone® chocolate bars.

Photo Provided

Greek Avgolemono Soup

serves 8

INGREDIENTS

8 cups chicken broth
3 medium eggs
½ cup rice
Juice from 2 lemons
Salt

Optional: scallions to top

Fred Smerlas

1180 WHAM RADIO SPORTS SHOW HOST
FORMER BUFFALO BILL

WHAT TO TOAST WITH

Nobilo
Marlborough
Sauvignon
Blanc

WHATCHA GOTTA DO...

Bring chicken broth to a boil. Salt to taste. Add rice to taste, cover, simmer 20 minutes. Remove from heat. In blender, beat 3 eggs, slowly add lemon juice to egg mixture. Add one cup of chicken broth while blending. When the broth and eggs are well mixed, pour back into remaining broth and rice. Stir well over heat, but do not allow to boil.

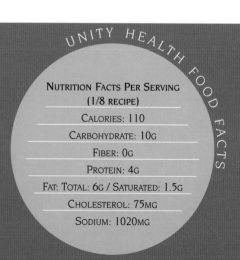

UNITY HEALTH FOOD FACTS

NUTRITION FACTS PER SERVING
(1/8 RECIPE)

CALORIES: 110

CARBOHYDRATE: 10G

FIBER: 0G

PROTEIN: 4G

FAT: TOTAL: 6G / SATURATED: 1.5G

CHOLESTEROL: 75MG

SODIUM: 1020MG

Gary Smith

1180 WHAM RADIO
TRAFFIC REPORTER

Why is this your favorite healthy entrée recipe?

I'd rather have regular meat lasagna, but I know this is healthier.

What is your fitness regime?

Golf, skiing, and working out with Nautilus equipment.

What is your secret food indulgence?

Chocolate chip cookies!

INGREDIENTS

2 10 oz. packages of frozen chopped
   spinach
8 oz. low-fat cottage cheese
¼ cup grated Parmesan cheese
32 oz. jar of meatless spaghetti
   sauce
½ cup dry red wine
¼ teaspoon garlic powder
⅛ teaspoon ground nutmeg
8 oz. sliced mozzarella cheese
1 cup sliced fresh mushrooms
Lasagna noodles

Vegetable Lasagna

serves 8

WHATCHA GOTTA DO...

Place spinach in a 2-quart glass dish. Microwave on high for 5-6 minutes. Drain and set aside. Stir in cottage cheese and Parmesan cheese and set aside. Combine spaghetti sauce, wine, garlic powder, and nutmeg in a 2-quart glass bowl. Cover with plastic wrap and microwave on high for 6-8 minutes or until hot. Remove 1 cup of sauce and set aside. Add spinach to sauce remaining in bowl. Layer lasagna as follows: half of spinach mixture, 4 noodles, half of cottage cheese, half of mozzarella cheese, half of mushrooms. Repeat layers, pour reserved cup of sauce over top. Cover and microwave on high for 6 minutes. Rotate dish and microwave on medium-high for 20 minutes.

WHAT TO TOAST WITH

Nobilo
Marlborough
Sauvignon
Blanc

NUTRITION FACTS PER SERVING
(1/4 RECIPE)

CALORIES: 850

CARBOHYDRATE: 45G

FIBER: 4G

PROTEIN: 42G

FAT: TOTAL: 54G / SATURATED: 21G

CHOLESTEROL: 240MG

SODIUM: 1430MG

WHAT TO TOAST WITH

Simi
Sonoma
Chardonnay

Tomato sauce with Shrimp and Feta

INGREDIENTS

serves 4-6

4 tablespoons olive oil

1 tablespoon garlic

2 cups Roma tomatoes, peeled and
   chopped

⅓ cup dry white wine

¼ cup chopped fresh basil

1 teaspoon oregano

30 medium shrimp

⅛ teaspoon crushed red pepper
   flakes

½ lb. Feta cheese

Pasta (penne or bowtie)

Shari Smith (& Emily!)

1180 WHAM RADIO
MORNING NEWS ANCHOR

Why is this your favorite healthy entrée recipe?

That question is pretty simple. Does it have shrimp in it? Well, then it is for me.

What is your fitness regime?

I walk. I run. I swim. (They look like sentences from a first grade reading book!)

What is your secret food indulgence?

Two words—JUNK FOOD! Chips, pretzels, etc.

WHATCHA GOTTA DO...

Heat 2 tablespoons oil over medium heat. Add garlic. Sauté for about 1 minute. Add tomatoes, cook for 2 minutes. Add wine, basil, and oregano and simmer for 10 minutes. Meanwhile, in medium pan, heat remaining oil and add the shrimp. Sauté 1 to 2 minutes. Sprinkle with red pepper. Add the shrimp to the tomato sauce and serve over pasta (I like to use penne or bowtie). Last, but not least, sprinkle on the Feta cheese and enjoy!

Cook time: All told, about 20 minutes to throw together.

119

Crockpot Herbed Turkey Breast

serves 4-6

INGREDIENTS

1 (5-6 lb.) turkey breast (boneless, skinless, thawed, trimmed)
2 tablespoons butter
¼ cup garden vegetable cream cheese
1 tablespoon soy sauce

1 tablespoon parsley
¼ teaspoon garlic powder
½ teaspoon each basil, sage, thyme, rosemary
Black pepper to taste

WHATCHA GOTTA DO...

Place turkey in crockpot. Combine remaining ingredients and brush or rub over turkey. Cover; cook on low 8-10 hours or high 4-6 hours (until turkey shreds apart). Serve over brown rice or mashed potatoes.

Cook time: Crockpot high temperature: 4-6 hrs; low temperature: 8-10 hrs.

WHAT TO TOAST WITH

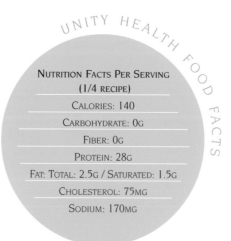

Banrock Station East Australian Shiraz

UNITY HEALTH FOOD FACTS

NUTRITION FACTS PER SERVING
(1/4 RECIPE)

CALORIES: 140

CARBOHYDRATE: 0G

FIBER: 0G

PROTEIN: 28G

FAT: TOTAL: 2.5G / SATURATED: 1.5G

CHOLESTEROL: 75MG

SODIUM: 170MG

Steve Tasker

1180 WHAM Radio Sports Show Host
Former Buffalo Bill

Why is this your favorite healthy entrée recipe?

There aren't very many entrees that our whole family agrees upon, but all five of our children, my wife, and I love this one. That makes it a big hit in the Tasker house. Plus, it's a delicious, hearty, low-fat, savory dish for those long, cold, winter nights.

What is your fitness regime?

In the winter I lift weights. In the warmer months, I golf every chance I get. (Golf counts as a fitness regime if you do it a lot, you skip the cart, and carry your bag.)

What is your secret food indulgence?

Buckets of popcorn and soda when I go to the movies.

Meredith's Apple Pie

INGREDIENTS

6 Granny Smith apples
3 Macintosh apples
1 box of Jiffy® crust mix
1 beaten egg white

1 cup of sugar
1 teaspoon of apple spice mix
1 pat of butter
1 beaten egg yolk

WHATCHA GOTTA DO...

Peel and chop the apples. Make pie crust with Jiffy® mix. Place crust in pie pan and brush crust with beaten egg whites. Dump apples into pie crust. Combine sugar and apple spice mix and sprinkle mixture on apples. Sprinkle sugar and apple spice mix on apples. Place pat of butter on top of the apples. Place top layer of crust over apples. Bake at 400 degrees for first 10 min. Bake at 350 for the next 35-40 min or until top of crust is brown.

UNITY HEALTH FOOD FACTS

NUTRITION FACTS PER SERVING
(1/8 RECIPE)

CALORIES: 430

CARBOHYDRATE: 68G

FIBER: 5G

PROTEIN: 4G

FAT: TOTAL: 17G / SATURATED: 4.5G

CHOLESTEROL: 30MG

SODIUM: 260MG

Meredith Viera

ABC TV's "The View" Co-Host

Chet's Chili

INGREDIENTS

3 tablespoons vegetable oil
3 stalks of celery
1 large onion, chopped
1 large green pepper, chopped
4 15 oz. cans Mexican-style stewed tomatoes
2 16 oz. cans pinto beans, drained
2 11 oz. can whole kernel corn, drained
1 4 oz. can diced green chilis
1 cup fresh cilantro, chopped
¼ cup chili powder
1 tablespoon ground cumin

WHATCHA GOTTA DO...

Heat oil in Dutch oven over high heat. Sauté celery, onion, bell pepper, and garlic until they begin to soften (about 8 minutes). Add all remaining ingredients except cilantro and simmer about 35 minutes. During the last 10 minutes, add cilantro. Serves a large family or one person for a week.

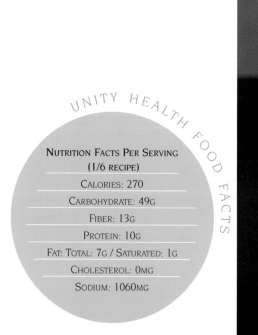

UNITY HEALTH FOOD FACTS

NUTRITION FACTS PER SERVING
(1/6 RECIPE)

CALORIES: 270

CARBOHYDRATE: 49G

FIBER: 13G

PROTEIN: 10G

FAT: TOTAL: 7G / SATURATED: 1G

CHOLESTEROL: 0MG

SODIUM: 1060MG

Chet Walker

1180 WHAM Radio,
Co-host, WHAM Morning News

Why is this your favorite healthy entrée recipe?

This was concocted when I was just out of college, broke, with no one to cook for me but Wendy and Ronald McDonald.

What is your fitness regime?

Jogging my memory, running my mouth, jumping to conclusions, leaps of faith, office yoga (bending over backwards, stretching the truth, and putting my foot in my mouth), throwing fits, dragging my feet, wading through paperwork! Seriously, jogging is what I enjoy doing although people who have seen me jog say it looks more like slow walking with a lot of huffing and puffing.

What is your secret food indulgence?

A certain dessert makes me want to tear off my clothes and roll around naked in it. I don't know the name of it, but it is a chocolate puff pastry filled with warm vanilla and drenched with hot chocolate sauce!

NUTRITION FACTS PER SERVING
(1/12 RECIPE)

CALORIES: 220

CARBOHYDRATE: 16G

FIBER: 6G

PROTEIN: 4G

FAT: TOTAL: 16G / SATURATED: 2.5G

CHOLESTEROL: 10MG

SODIUM: 380MG

WHAT TO TOAST WITH

Estancia
Pinot
Grigio

Betty's Potato Salad

serves 6 as a side

INGREDIENTS

5 *lbs. potatoes*
1 *cup Hellmann's® mayonnaise*
2 *tablespoons lemon juice*
2 *tablespoons sugar*
1 *teaspoon salt*
6 *cups shredded cabbage*
2 *slices of ham (chopped into
    small pieces)*
2 *tablespoons sour cream*

Patrice Walsh

13WHAM NEWS REPORTER

Why is this your favorite healthy entrée recipe?

This recipe comes from my mother, Betty Walsh, who has been making what we consider the best potato salad for 50 years. She is a terrific cook and teacher and taught me everything she knows about cooking (although I admit I'm not a big cook!).

What is your fitness regime?

Running around with three teenagers, following and/or ferrying them to sporting events, and other activities—we're always on the go! I also do regular exercise, walk the dog, as well as running around covering stories every day!

What is your secret food indulgence?

Chocolate, not that I indulge that much. But it is definitely a favorite!

WHATCHA GOTTA DO...

Boil, peel, and cut potatoes into small pieces. Add ingredients, in order shown, and mix. Chill until ready to serve. (You may also substitute light mayonnaise.)

Barbara Walters

ABC TV's "The View" Co-Host

INGREDIENTS

3 lbs. lean ground chuck

Salt to taste

¾ teaspoon pepper

2 teaspoons celery salt (or to taste)

½ cup ketchup

2 eggs

½ cup crushed, unsalted crackers

2 heads green cabbage
(2 lbs. each)

6 quarts boiling water

3 cups chopped onion

2 bottles chili sauce (12 oz. each)

1 12 oz. jar grape jelly

¼ cup water

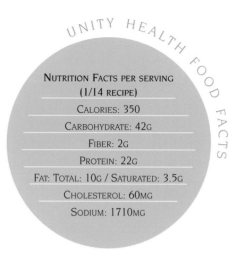

serves 14

Barbara Walters' Mother's Stuffed Cabbage Rolls

WHATCHA GOTTA DO...

Preheat oven to 375. In a large bowl, combine meat, salt, pepper, celery salt, ketchup, eggs, and crackers. Mix with your hands until mixture is well combined. Cut out and discard hard center core of cabbage. Place cabbage in a large kettle. Pour 6 quarts boiling water over it. Let stand until leaves are flexible and can be easily removed from the head (about 5 minutes). If necessary, return cabbage to hot water to soften inner leaves. Drain cabbage leaves. Using a ¼ cup measure, scoop up a scant ¼ cup of the meat mixture. With your hands, form into rolls, 3" long and 1" wide. Place each meat roll on a drained cabbage leaf. Fold top of leaf over meat, then fold in sides and roll up into an oblong shape. Continue rolling remaining meat rolls in cabbage leaves. You'll make about 28 rolls total. In bottom of a lightly greased 11½ x 12 x 2¼ inch roasting pan, spread chopped onion evenly. Arrange cabbage rolls in neat rows on top of onion. In a 2-quart saucepan, combine chili sauce, grape jelly, and ¼ cup water. Heat over medium heat, stirring, till jelly melts. Pour over cabbage rolls. Cover pan tightly with foil. Bake in preheated 375 oven for 2 hours. Remove foil. Brush rolls with sauce. Continue baking, uncovered, another 40 minutes or until sauce is thick and syrupy, and cabbage rolls are glazed. Serve with sauce spooned over them.

WHAT TO TOAST WITH

Nobilo
Marlborough
Sauvignon
Blanc

Honey Pecan Chicken

INGREDIENTS

1 cup Wheat Chex® cereal crumbs
⅓ cup finely chopped pecans
2 tablespoons honey
2 tablespoons low-sodium soy sauce
6 skinless, boneless chicken breasts
Salt and pepper to taste

WHATCHA GOTTA DO...

Preheat the oven to 425 degrees. Cover a baking sheet with foil and spray with nonstick cooking spray. On a plate or on waxed paper, combine the cereal crumbs and pecans. In a bowl, mix together the honey and soy sauce. Season the chicken with salt and pepper. Dip both sides of the chicken breast into the honey mixture; then roll in the pecan mixture to coat. Arrange the chicken on the pan. Bake for 12-15 minutes on each side or until the chicken is done. Serve.

Christine Webb

13WHAM NEWS HEALTH TEAM REPORTER

Why is this your favorite healthy entrée recipe?

I love making this for company. Many people just don't think that healthy can be tasty and delicious; this is sweet and crunchy and is a different twist to chicken

What is your fitness regime?

My fitness regime! I love training for Ironmans—the most grueling triathlons in the world. An Ironman is a 2.4 mile swim, 112 mile bike ride and running a marathon of 26.2 miles. I probably log about 20 hours a week on exercise. I'm up at 4 or 5 am swimming, running, or biking for a couple of hours. Then at night, it's a combination of running and biking for a couple of hours. I also love yoga and Pilates—other good fitness challenges! I've taken part in 100-mile bike rides for charity and have run 12 marathons. I'm also on a masters swim team.

What is your secret food indulgence?

My favorite secret food indulgence would have to be chocolate raspberry cheesecake. Once in a blue moon, if I've been training really hard, I will indulge myself with a small piece of this heavenly delight!

NUTRITION FACTS PER SERVING
(1/6 RECIPE)

CALORIES: 320

CARBOHYDRATE: 11G

FIBER: 1G

PROTEIN: 45G

FAT: TOTAL: 10G / SATURATED: 2G

CHOLESTEROL: 120MG

SODIUM: 330MG

WHAT TO TOAST WITH

Nobilo
Marlborough
Sauvignon
Blanc

NUTRITION FACTS PER SERVING
(1/4 RECIPE)

CALORIES: 605

CARBOHYDRATE: 14G

FIBER: 3G

PROTEIN: 65G

FAT: TOTAL: 31G / SATURATED: 15G

CHOLESTEROL: 250MG

SODIUM: 1750MG

WHAT TO TOAST WITH

Blackstone
California
Merlot

Whit's Pork Tenderloin

Mike Whittemore

1180 WHAM RADIO TALK SHOW HOST
ACCOUNT EXECUTIVE

Why is this your favorite healthy entrée recipe?

It's quick and easy. Pork tenderloin has really become my favorite meat of ANY kind.

What is your fitness regime?

THAT is the challenge of my life. I truly enjoy working up a sweat. I love the stair climbers and elliptical machines at the Bayview YMCA, as well as Nautilus. Now…if I only had the discipline to go more frequently.

What is your secret food indulgence?

If one of the top three ingredients is sugar, it is certain to find its way into my mouth!

INGREDIENTS

Pork Tenderloins
2 *generous-sized pork tenderloins*
Emeril's Southwest Seasoning
  (generous portion for rub)

Horseradish Sauce
2 *cups light sour cream*
1/3 *cup Rollers® prepared horseradish,*
  drained (from Palmers)
1 *tablespoon minced chives*
1 *teaspoon fresh lime juice*
1 *teaspoon salt*
Dash hot red pepper sauce

WHATCHA GOTTA DO…

I love to cook. I'm a big fan of the Food Channel and even bigger fan of Emeril Lagasse. In fact, when he was in town several years ago, I actually stood in line at a local bookstore for five and a half hours to have a book signed and chat with him for a grand total of fifteen seconds.

I guess I will feed the stereotype that "guys only grill" with the following offering: Get your Weber charcoal grill nice and hot (I'll NEVER use a gas grill because I'm absolutely certain if I did, I'd find a way to blow myself up). When the grill is heating, take a couple of nice-size pork tenderloins out of the package and season them liberally with Emeril's Southwest Seasoning. (I used to make my own fresh from one of his cookbooks, but have since given into the convenience of the bottles on the shelf at the grocery store). Throw the pork tenderloin on the grill a few minutes a side directly over the hot coals to seal in the juices. Once they're nicely browned, move them off the direct heat, put the top on and finish cooking. (If they're on the grill more than fifteen minutes total, you're overcooking them, but use your best judgment). Take the tenderloins off the grill and let them rest for about ten minutes before slicing them into glorious little medallions. You've cooked them perfectly if there's still some pink in the middle (no really…it won't kill you). The meat will generate some really tasty juice, but for the purposes of this cookbook, you can also whip up the quick-and-easy horseradish sauce from the ingredients above.

NUTRITION FACTS PER SERVING
(2 TRUFFLES)

CALORIES: 150

CARBOHYDRATE: 14G

FIBER: 1G

PROTEIN: 1G

FAT: TOTAL: 10G / SATURATED: 6G

CHOLESTEROL: 20MG

SODIUM: 10MG

WHAT TO TOAST WITH

Banrock
Station
South East
Australian
Shiraz

Dark Chocolate Mint Truffles

INGREDIENTS

7 oz. good quality dark sweet chocolate
½ cup whipping (35%) cream
1½ teaspoon crème de menthe
1 teaspoon peppermint extract
Good quality cocoa powder, for rolling

Barry Vee

1180 WHAM Radio Traffic Reporter

**Why is this your favorite healthy
entrée recipe?**
Chocolate! Need I say more?!

What is your fitness regime?
I walk and run regularly.

What is your secret food indulgence?
Anything with chocolate (dark chocolate is good
too!). I also enjoy fresh strawberries with angel
food cake and whipped cream.

WHATCHA GOTTA DO...

Chop the chocolate very finely and transfer to medium bowl. Boil cream and immediately pour over chopped chocolate. Stir until all chocolate has melted. Stir in crème de menthe and peppermint extract until blended. Cover surface with plastic wrap and freeze until firm (about 2 hours). Scoop into small balls with melon baller and transfer to a baking sheet. Freeze for 10 minutes. Roll truffles in cocoa powder.

How to Lighten Up Our Celebrity Favorites

Although nutritionists agree that all foods fit, some foods fit special diets better than others. If you are watching your weight, cholesterol, blood sugar or blood pressure, you might want to modify some of the recipes in this cookbook.

Watching Your Weight?

- Check out the portion size. In many of these recipes, portions are generous, so a small serving might suit you better.

- Ideally, produce should take up about half your plate. Add volume to your meal with a second vegetable, salad or cut up fresh fruits and veggies.

- Cutting the fat often makes a dent in calorie content without a noticeable change in the recipe.

- Use half the oil called for in most entrée dishes.

- Try reduced fat or lite cheese and low fat milk.

- Trim meat of fat and chicken of skin before cooking.

Curbing Cholesterol?

Animal fat is the main source of artery-clogging saturated fat (the material your body uses to make "bad" cholesterol) in our diet. Here are tips to cut meat and dairy fats:

- Trim meats well before cooking.

- Drain accumulated fat after browning ground beef.

- Use fat-free milk and low-fat cheeses in place of regular.

- Switch to tub margarine in recipes calling for butter.

- Compromise! Use half butter and half margarine or olive oil, depending on the recipe. Or try a butter canola blend.

Shaking the Salt Habit

Using less salt at the table and in your cooking helps, so where possible, omit the added salt. Most of the sodium in our diet comes from processed foods. You can lighten the sodium in recipes by changing processed ingredients:

- Use garlic or onion powder instead of garlic or onion salt.

- Drain and rinse canned beans.

- Select lower sodium or lite soups, stocks, soy sauce, and salad dressings.

- Liven up vegetables and salads with a squeeze of fresh lemon juice or dash of balsamic vinegar.

Dodging Diabetes

- Watching your weight and getting regular exercise go a long way in preventing diabetes. To better control blood sugars, aim for higher fiber foods rich in unprocessed carbohydrates.

- Replace white rice with brown rice.

- Try the many bean-based and vegetable dishes in this cookbook.

- Use whole-wheat pastas.

- Check out the "watching your weight" section.

For more advice on how to enjoy your favorite foods on a special diet, contact the nutritionists at Unity Diabetes, Nutrition & Weight Management Center at (585) 254-4152.

Heron Hill Winery

Whole Grain Mustard-Crusted Halibut with Citrus Butter Sauce

This rich citrus sauce adds zest to halibut or any kind of firm white fish. Complement the meal with a glass of Heron Hill's Eclipse White wine, an exotic blend of Pinot Gris, Chardonnay, and Sauvignon Blanc grapes.

INGREDIENTS

ROASTED HALIBUT
1 cup whole grain prepared mustard
2 tablespoons Dijon mustard
2 tablespoons minced garlic
1/4 cup Heron Hill Eclipse White wine
1 1/2 lbs. Halibut fillet

CITRUS BUTTER SAUCE
2 cups Heron Hill Eclipse White wine
Zest of 1 orange
Zest of 1 lemon
Zest of 1 lime
2 tablespoons heavy cream
2 sticks salted butter, cut into
    1 tablespoon pieces
Salt

HERON HILL ECLIPSE
WHITE WINE

Combine the whole grain and Dijon mustard, garlic, and wine. Trim any skin from the fish and cut into four equal fillets. Place in small roasting pan without crowding. Spread equal amount of mustard mixture evenly over the top of each fillet. Cover and let rest for 15 minutes. Roast halibut 8 to 10 minutes or until just done. Put fish on four plates, pour sauce over, and serve.

While the fish roasts, prepare the sauce. Bring wine and citrus zests to a boil in a medium saucepan then lower the heat until the wine mixture simmers. Reduce wine mixture by half. Add cream and simmer 5 minutes. Remove saucepan from heat and whip in butter, one piece at a time until all is mixed in. Taste and add salt as desired. Hold at room temperature and do not reheat.

Wine Mushroom Sauce

Serve this flavorful sauce with beef, lamb, veal, or venison. Pair with a glass of Heron Hill's full-bodied Eclipse Red wine to complete your meal.

INGREDIENTS

Two dozen mushrooms, sliced
Two sticks butter or margarine
1 tablespoon chopped onion
1/2 teaspoon black pepper
2 tablespoons lemon juice
1/2 cup cornstarch
1 1/2 teaspoon salt
1 tablespoon Worcestershire Sauce
1 tablespoon parsley flakes
2 cups water
2 cups Heron Hill
    Eclipse Red wine

HERON HILL ECLIPSE
RED WINE

Sauté and brown mushrooms in mixture of butter, onion, pepper, salt, lemon juice, Worcestershire Sauce, and parsley. Remove mushrooms from pan (by straining). Add water and wine to the pan drippings. When mixture boils, add the cornstarch that has been dissolved in a small amount of water. Whisk to make gravy of desired thickness (a thin consistency is better). Return mushrooms to pan. More wine may be added just before serving to add more zip!

Serves four.

The Natural Choice

The brands under the LiDestri family of sauces are a natural way to make every meal a tasteful experience. *Francesco Rinaldi Pasta Sauces* feature only the finest tomatoes, imported Pecorino Romano cheese, imported extra virgin olive oil and just the right blend of herbs and spices.

Santa Fe Salsa and Con Queso are perfect with nachos, tortilla chips and right at home on eggs or as a filling for omelettes. Try it on grilled pork, chicken or fish.

LiDestri Foods Finishing Sauces are the perfect complement to your proteins. A great fit with chicken, beef, veal, pork or fish. These unique sauces are ready to use right out of the jar, or add your own special touches to create a signature sauce all your own.

Francesco Rinaldi Pasta Sauces, Santa Fe Salsa and Con Queso and LiDestri Finishing Sauces are made with the highest level of quality ingredients mixed with old-world knowledge to deliver the best to you and your family.

Finishing Sauce

www.francescorinaldi.com

As Good as it Gets!

www.santafepackingcompany.com

UnToppable Quality since 1925

It began in the Roaring Twenties, when Nance Delmarle created something extraordinary in her Upstate New York kitchen – a Sharp & Creamy mustard unlike any other. It wasn't long until she was impressing her neighbors with other new condiments, including her Chicken Wing Sauce, Chili Sauce and Corn Relish. Today, you can still enjoy sauces based on Nance's original recipes. Discover the UnToppable Quality of Nance's for yourself and share it with others!

Authentic Hot Wing Recipe

2 to 2-1/2 pounds chicken wings
1/2 cup Nance's Hot Wing Sauce
Celery sticks
Blue Cheese Dressing

Makes about twenty-four

Heat oven to 400°F. Place chicken wings in 13 x 9-inch baking pan. Bake, uncovered for 50 to 60 minutes, or until fully cooked, turning once. Toss with Nance's Wing Sauce and bake 5 minutes longer. Serve warm with celery sticks and blue cheese dressing, if desired.

* Top off chicken sandwiches or appetizers with Nance's Hot Wing Sauce.

An UnToppable Tradition

Since 1916, dessert lovers have consistently craved the UnToppable taste of Mrs. Richardson's toppings. These velvety-smooth products not only raise the dessert bar, they sit atop it! Indulge yourself in the sweet spectrum of Mrs. Richardson's flavors. You can even do it without guilt, thanks to our fat-free varieties. Top off your desserts with Mrs. Richardson's UnToppable Quality.

Fudge Pecan Pie

Serves 8

1 cup light corn syrup
3 packets Mrs. Richardson's Hot Fudge Topping*
1/4 cup firmly packed light brown sugar
1/4 cup (1/2 stick) butter, melted and cooled
3 eggs, slightly beaten
2 tablespoons all-purpose flour

1 teaspoon vanilla extract
1-1/2 cups pecan halves
One 9-inch unbaked pie shell
Whipped cream
Pecan halves

Heat oven to 325°F. Combine corn syrup, Mrs. Richardson's Hot Fudge topping, brown sugar, butter, eggs, flour and vanilla in large bowl. Mix until well blended. Stir in pecan halves. Pour mixture into unbaked pie shell and bake 55 to 65 minutes or until crust is golden brown and knife inserted in center comes out clean. Cool completely. Top with whip cream and pecan halves on each slice.

* May substitute with Mrs. Richardson's Chocolate Lover's Topping.
Also great with warmed Mrs. Richardson's Butterscotch Caramel drizzled over top!

Santos Demoiselle Watch *Cartier*

2945 MONROE AVENUE • ROCHESTER, NY 14618
585-271-4000 • 800-828-6234
WWW.MANNSJEWELERS.COM

140

MacKenzie-Childs Cookware

HOME DESIGNS WITH THE PERSONAL TOUCH

Kitchens that are airy and sunlit, entranceways that are both dramatic and welcoming, spacious living rooms that reflect a personal style—custom designs, created around your dreams and within your budget.

At Ketmar, our designers work with you to capture your vision, from the initial floor plan to the final landscaping, creating a home that's as unique as you.

But with Ketmar, you'll do more than build a home. You'll build a legacy—with individualized design, timeless craftsmanship, and inspiring architecture that will live with your family for generations to come.

IT'S THE KETMAR DIFFERENCE.

Ketmar
Development Corporation

2 Epping Wood Trail   Pittsford, New York   (585) 381-7758   www.Ketmar.com

AT THE HEART OF YOUR HOME...

No room in your home says as much about you as your kitchen. Centrally located and abuzz with activity, your kitchen showcases *your* style, *your* attention to detail, *your* passion for living.

Custom kitchen designer Kim Martin brings over twenty years of customer-focused experience to each project. With her eclectic team of interior designers and seasoned remodelers, Kim works with each homeowner, listening to their needs, giving form to their dreams, creating an inviting space that's so integral to the home.

A full service, design-build firm, Custom Kitchens by Martin & Co. delivers the knowledge, experience, and craftsmanship your home deserves, ensuring your kitchen is truly *your* kitchen.

Custom Kitchens by Martin & Co. Inc.   Pittsford, NY   (585) 383-1388   By appointment only.

Rocky Mountain

GRANITE & MARBLE INC.

Rocky Mountain Granite & Marble Inc., established in 1996, has one of the largest selections of granite in upstate New York. We have stone from Italy, Spain, Norway, Brazil and from other countries from around the world. Our stock of over 1,800 slabs in hundreds of colors and styles is what makes us the number one choice in the area.

All of our inventory can be viewed at our facility where the client can select a stone that compliments their taste and design. Our inventory consists of popular and common material, as well as unique and rare pieces of stone, granite, marble, soapstone, travertine, limestone, and onyx.

Our staff with over 25 years of experience is ready to assist you in choosing the color of your choice, making your decision process easy. Whether it's the old look feel or something contemporary, we have the material you desire.

Rocky Mountain Granite & Marble Inc.
720 Basket Road
Webster NY 14580
585.265.6610

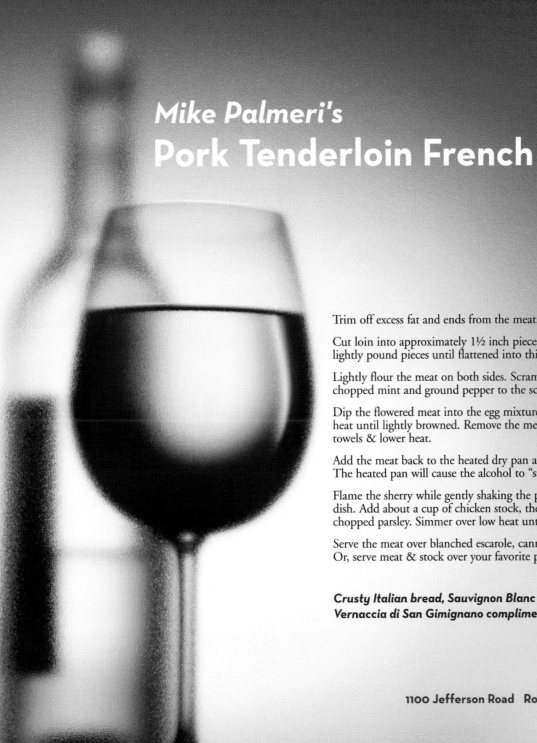

Mike Palmeri's
Pork Tenderloin French

this dish can be made with chicken, veal, fish, artichoke hearts or eggplant.

1 package pork tenderloins (usually two/package)
1 cup all-purpose flour
2-3 eggs
½ cup grated Pecorino Romano or Parmesan cheese
1 tablespoon chopped mint leaves
1 tablespoon chopped parsley
½ teaspoon ground black pepper
1 lemon
2-3 tablespoons olive oil or vegetable oil
2-3 cloves finely chopped garlic
1 bunch escarole rinsed and chopped
6-8 pitted and chopped Italian or Greek cured olives
4-6 pats of butter
½ cup Amontillado (medium dry) sherry
1 cup chicken stock
1 cup cannelloni beans

Trim off excess fat and ends from the meat.

Cut loin into approximately 1½ inch pieces. Turn on cut side and between 2 pieces of waxed paper; lightly pound pieces until flattened into thin pieces (about ¼ thick)

Lightly flour the meat on both sides. Scramble 2 or 3 eggs and add about ½ cup of grated pecorino romano cheese, chopped mint and ground pepper to the scrambled eggs.

Dip the flowered meat into the egg mixture and coat both sides. Sautée the meat in olive or vegetable oil over medium heat until lightly browned. Remove the meat from the pan and drain on paper towels. Wipe out the pan with paper towels & lower heat.

Add the meat back to the heated dry pan and our about a ½ cup of Amontillado (medium dry) sherry over the meat. The heated pan will cause the alcohol to "steam" off. Use a long match to light the fumes.

Flame the sherry while gently shaking the pan. The alcohol will burn off, and the flavor of the wine will enhance the dish. Add about a cup of chicken stock, the juice of one lemon and 4-6 pats of butter. Sprinkle with grated cheese and chopped parsley. Simmer over low heat until ready to plate.

Serve the meat over blanched escarole, cannelloni beans and pitted Italian olives sautéed in garlic infused olive oil. Or, serve meat & stock over your favorite pasta.

Crusty Italian bread, Sauvignon Blanc or Vernaccia di San Gimignano compliments the dish.

DELL'S HOUSE OF KITCHENS, INC.

Rochester's Leading Kitchen Specialist for 50 Years

3445 Winton Place
At The Design Center
Rochester, NY 14623
(585) 272-1840

Homemade Salsa

1 can stewed tomatoes
1 can "Rotel" tomatoes
½ chopped green pepper
½ small red onion chopped
1 tablespoon chopped garlic

1 tablespoon cumin
Juice of ½ a lime
Salt and pepper to taste
Handful fresh cilantro leaves, minced

Put all ingredients in a blender. Chop and pulse until it's the consistency you like. Pour in a bowl and serve right away. If you're brave and want it a little hotter, add a dash of cayenne pepper or jalapeno.

Celebrity Index